INVESTING FOR PLEASURE AND PROFIT

by
JOHN PETERSON

DOW JONES BOOKS
PRINCETON, NEW JERSEY

Dow Jones Books and the author wish to express their appreciation for the valued contributions to INVESTING FOR PLEASURE AND PROFIT made by the copyright holders below.

Quotations from the work, THE COLLECTING MAN, by John Bedford. Published in 1967 by David McKay Co., Inc. Reprinted by permission of the publisher.

Quotations from the book, THE ART CROWD, by Sophy Burnham. Copyright ©1973 by Sophy Burnham. Published by David McKay Co., Inc. Reprinted by permission of the publisher.

Quotations from the books, ART AS AN INVESTMENT and ANTIQUES AS AN INVESTMENT, by Richard H. Rush. Copyright ©1968 by Richard H. Rush. Published by Prentice-Hall, Inc., Englewood Cliffs, NJ. Reprinted by permission of the publisher.

Quotations from the book, THE ELEGANT AUCTIONEERS, by Wesley Towner. Reprinted with the permission of Hill and Wang (a division of Farrar, Straus & Giroux, Inc.) Copyright © 1970 by the Estate of Wesley Towner.

Quotations from Coin World Magazine regarding the Bowers and Ruddy Auction is reprinted with the permission of Coin World, Sidney, Ohio.

Quotations from the book, THE ART OF THE FAKER, by Frank Arnau, published by Little, Brown and Company. Reprinted by permission of the author's agent, Pat Feeley.

Published by Dow Jones Books
P.O. Box 300, Princeton, NJ 08540

Printed and bound in the United States of America
10 9 8 7 6 5 4 3 2

Library of Congress Cataloging in Publication Data

Peterson, John, 1939-
Investing for pleasure and profit.

1. Collectors and collecting—Handbooks, manuals, etc.
2. Investments—Handbooks, manuals, etc.
I. Title.
AM231.P47 658 77-5800
ISBN 0-87128-509-6

Introduction

Profit. Pleasure. Profit and pleasure. The two do mix, and they mix quite well.

Just how they can be mixed—and the benefits and rewards that such a mixture can involve—are what this book is all about. As John Peterson shows, there is no oil-and-water effect when it comes to acquiring things of special value, watching them increase in worth and all the while experiencing the warm glow of pleasure that can come from appreciation of beautiful things. In fact, quite the opposite of an oil-and-water effect occurs. The people who discuss their experiences in this book, those who have tried it and done it, know that investing in the right things at the right time can produce both profit and pleasure. Enriching. Financially and otherwise.

With a cautious approach and a careful eye, practically everyone can participate in collecting almost anything—be it rare violins, old oak tables, gold coins or royal jewels. The list of items that can be collected for both profit and pleasure is nearly endless. It is limited only by one's imagination and foresight.

The rewards can be manifold. As John Peterson illustrates, prudent investing in collectibles can accomplish many things. For instance, a well-considered investment in, say, stamps, can help protect an investor from having his wealth eroded by inflation. It can also mean, on occasion, an unexpected thrill. The reason is that almost overnight values for some collectibles can soar, sometimes reaching levels that no one ever dreamed would be possible.

At the same time, the risks are many. If you hope to receive maximum benefit from reading *Investing for Pleasure and Profit,* you will have to understand—and appreciate—the phrase "caveat emptor."

"Caveat emptor" appears often in this book. It

means "let the purchaser beware" (let the buyer examine the article, and act on his own judgment at his own risk) and it was as pertinent to the business-like field of English Common Law which emphasized the maxim, as it will be to you in studying the ideas and suggestions John Peterson describes. Again and again we are reminded: to buy and sell, successfully, properties of any type, you must know your subject. You must understand every facet—origin, condition, authenticity, comparable properties, values, competitive market places, trends and countless other aspects.

At the same time, experts, such as the appraisers, collectors and dealers quoted by the author, stress the deep importance of experiencing pleasure in the pursuit of our "investments." Too much emphasis cannot be placed upon the importance of deriving real satisfaction from *the process* of buying and selling itself and from the intangible but equally real joy of collecting objects that bring a new perspective, a new and vital viewpoint to life.

I suppose, therefore, it might be effective if we thought of "caveat emptor" as one side of an evenly-balanced scale, and "ars gratia artis" (art for the sake of art) on the other.

So, goes the theme of this book: be knowledgeable, and enjoy the exercise of that knowledge through an orderly, disciplined, cumulative process. If you succeed, you will have the best of both worlds.

Perhaps you will better understand, and more completely enjoy this book if you know a bit about the "input" made by some of the experts. Let me describe one aspect.

Mr. Peterson wrote to all of the appraisers in the United States who are tested and certified professionals in their special branch of the world of Personal Property Appraisals (there are such recognized categories as Antiques, Fine Arts, Gems and Jewelry, Residential Contents, together with such specialties as coins, stamps, antique cars, etc.). The American Society of Appraisers cooperated informally with this research effort. We were as interested in the replies to the questionnaire as was Mr. Peterson.

In working with his materials, the author has cut to the bone, and applied with relevance, the story of investment for pleasure and profit. The ideas and experiences of experts are pointed directly to anyone who will listen: pleasure and profit can be integrated successfully by a thoughtful practitioner.

There is an additional aspect of this book that may be of benefit to many readers. It has been my experience—in observing and working with professionally-oriented collectors and dealers of personal property, as well as other professionals in fields of insurance, taxation, law and investment counselling—that many collectors, hobbyists, and dealers possess unusual expertise in value concepts, perceptions and practice. They have earned this expertise through hard work, patient observation, continuous study. And now, with John Peterson's book, their expertise can be shared.

It is a pleasure to introduce this book to both the "old hand" and "beginner" in the exciting world of investing, collecting, buying and selling and appraising personal properties. Quotations from the experts give substance to the pages. Diversity of opinions, backgrounds, experiences and concepts gives the substance life and relevance. It is equally pleasurable to reflect upon the fact pointed out in the Commentary on Personal Property Appraisal (a guidebook which has special relevance to values of antiques, fine arts, gems and jewelry, residential contents) "through peoples' collecting activities thousands of significant vestiges of past times and cultures have not been lost. These accumulations bring beauty, history, enlightenment and pleasure to people . . ."

DEXTER D. MACBRIDE, FASA, FSVA
Reston, Virginia

Acknowledgements

Not only is there a cloak of mystery and wonder about great art, there's something about any work of art or craftsmanship that adds dimension to our lives. Many of us spend lifetimes courting art, probing into its meaning, hoping to enrich our lives through insight and vision. We all need mentors, advisors, and teachers, and we all seek to expand what we know of art, what quality gives a certain work immense value. George Bernard Shaw recognized that ability in certain men and described it as "the wise eye."

We have witnessed, just this decade, an explosion in the interest and demand for art, for aging objects of fine craftsmanship, for nearly anything that's either extraordinary or exceptionally beautiful. Since 1970 the number of shops that cater to collectors has tripled. The number of knowledgeable and wise experts, who know value and recognize quality, remains small. The reason: It requires great years of experience to accumulate the eye to detect the faked or forged item, the inexact reproduction, and most importantly, the shades of difference between the truly fine works and the passable relic.

This book is based on the knowledge of dozens of the most reputable and noted experts in the different areas of collecting. With their guidance there becomes a process to be pursued or a path to be followed from which both the experienced and the beginning collector can profit. These people have written dozens of books, which have sold millions of copies, appraised the nation's finest collections, bought and sold the best of antiques, objects of art, firearms, and musical instruments, to list a few of the dozens of categories. Their candor, their effort, and their willingness to discuss the "secrets" of their profession or avocation made my task of trying to order their information rewarding and hugely enjoyable. It is their expertise that makes this book of value, and if there may be an misrepresentation or error, the fault lies in my reportorial abilities. They are:

Winslow Ames, drawings, ceramics, antique furniture, Founderstown, R.I.

George Bensley, fine arts and antiques, Santa Ana, Calif.

Q. David Bowers, numismatics, Los Angeles.

Nate Bradlin, stringed instruments, Beachwood, O.

Juanita C. Brown, fine arts, Oklahoma City.

Catherine Bullowa, numismatics, Philadelphia, Pa.

Ruth N. Burns, antiques, porcelains, pottery, Shawnee Mission, Ks.

Stefan A. Cavallo, personal property, New York City.

James H. Cohen, numismatics, New Orleans, La.

Mervyn Cohn, gems, San Francisco.

Jeanne Coles, antiques, Belmont, Calif.

Lowell Collins, fine arts, Houston.

Henry K. Cordier, fine arts, personal property, Los Angeles.

Warren Cox, Eastern art, New York City.

William Croker, collectibles, Grundy Center, Iowa.

Robert Dalrymple, antique furniture, Ventura, Calif.

J. Lee Drexler, fine arts, gems, antiques, New York City

Lyle Downey, stringed instruments, fine arts, Santa Clara, Calif.

Raymond Fenster, gems, Brooklyn.

Marty Flaherty, antique jewelry and gems, Los Angeles

Thelma Fletcher, rare books, Salado, Texas.

Stephen Foster, paintings, San Francisco.

Seymour Freeman, gems, Scottsdale, Ariz.

June Fritch, antiques, objects of art, Scottsdale, Ariz.

Herman Herst, Jr., philately, Boca Raton, Fla.

Gerry Hiatt, antique tools and furniture, scientific and nautical instruments, Noblesville, Ind.

Margaret Hilmes, fine arts, Orientalia, Shawnee Mission, Ks.

F. Herbert Hoover, paintings, San Francisco

Warren Howell, rare books, San Francisco
Gertrude Tatnall Jacobson, antiques, Albuquerque, N.M.
Harold Jaffe, fine arts, personal property, Great Neck, N.Y.
Robert J. Kaller, paintings, sculpture, fine arts, Carmel, Calif.
John P. Klep, fine arts, paintings, Houston
Frank Knight, antiques, collectibles, numismatics, Kermit, Texas
Ralph and Terry Kovel, antiques, collectibles, Terre Haute, Ind.
William Lutton, antique furniture, San Francisco
George F. Manley, antiques, geological and archeological specimens, Wallingford, Conn.
John Mayhill, antiques, collectibles, Knightstown, Ind.
Phil Moran, fine arts, San Antonio, Texas
Tim Morrow, Oriental art, jade, pearls, Lahaina, Hawaii
George Musser, fine arts, Harrisburg, Pa.
Ruth Murphy, antiques, Lansing, Mich.
Majorie Neikrug, fine arts, New York City
Elsie Pease, antiques, Fort Worth, Texas
Alex Sabbadini, antiques and collectibles, Sacramento, Calif.
Lee Schreiber, antiques, Rosemont, Pa.
Ronald Schwarz, fine arts, home furnishings, San Francisco.
Dick Seelinger, antique and modern firearms, Cuyahoga Falls, O.
Donald R. Thompson, fire arms, Indian art, contemporary Western art, El Paso, Texas
John Tucker, paintings, Houston
Arlene Whalen, porcelains, antiques, European and Oriental art, San Diego, Calif.
B. Crosby Willet, art glass, Philadelphia, Pa.
James Willis, African art, San Francisco.
Frank Zoglin, fine arts, antiques, Kansas City, Mo.

An old saw holds that if man finds work that intrigues him, money will find a way into his pocket. These folks prove that theory. Not only do most possess that *joie de vivre* that comes with a fascinating profession, most are at least possessors of valuable collections and some are indeed wealthy. They meet the test: If they know so much why are they working and why aren't they quite wealthy? Well, most are quite wealthy and most are working because it pleases them to handle the finest works of art in their fields.

I also wish to thank Dexter MacBride and the members of the American Society of Appraisers, Nancy Jarvis, a research-interviewer with extraordinary ability and insight, and my editors at Dow Jones, Lionel Linder, Bill Giles, and Everett Groseclose.

Contents

Pick Your Niche

"Collecting," says appraiser William Lutton, "is a joyful pursuit because of the beauty it brings into a persons's life. But collecting becomes even more rewarding when you make some money at it."

This book is about pleasure and profit. It's also about protecting your capital against inflation and, in many instances, against either a jumbled economy or a recession. Hard data suggest the shrewd and capable collector is well prepared to weather very nearly any economic storm.

The best way to make money—whether in the stock market or in real estate—is to know more than other people. That holds true in collecting too. There's no sure way to turn a profit on any transaction, of course, but there is a process or procedure that experts agree shows handsome results. It turns on the assumption that any person can find an area of collecting that fascinates him so much that he'll be forever reading, researching, bargain hunting, inspecting, browsing, handling the merchandise, buying, trading, selling.

Simply put, all you do is buy the best—you can afford—of the rarest gems, coins, furniture, classic cars, Persian rugs, Samurai swords, paintings, glassware, figurines, stamps, books, clocks—and at a fair price. Then you wait as values increase. It doesn't take long, not with the manner in which the collectors' markets have been running in the 1970s. Millions of people are making big bucks.

In the past couple of years jade has tripled in value and diamonds have jumped by 250 per cent. Antique clocks and music boxes have doubled in the past year. Rare books and antique furniture have been increasing in value by 30 per cent annually. One collection of paintings by old masters increased to a current appraisal of $3 million, up from $100,000 in 1964. Of the 20 known 1876 20-cent pieces, one sold for $9,750 in 1961 and another went for $59,000 in 1974.

A person can either attempt to play the wise investor in this market, or he can play the plunger, the speculator. For example, one appraiser-dealer in San Antonio decided that Depression glass—that garishly gaudy crystal that service stations gave away to customers back in the 1930s—would become a collectible of value. That was half a dozen years ago. He collected more than 20,000 pieces at a cost of a few thousand dollars. Today, his collection is valued at nearly $200,000.

But don't figure that it's shooting clay pigeons with a shotgun, even though the experts contend this collectors' market will keep right on booming. This kind of investing demands patience, shrewdness, a hard-bargaining and calculating mind, knowledge won through hard work and study, and, naturally, "the wise eye."

It is a process and it means that you can take your hobby, avocation, or area of fascination and turn it into a business or at least a lucrative way of whiling away leisure time. Finally, you become an expert, a person who recognizes value and authenticity. Then, perhaps with some formal education, you could also become an author, dealer, appraiser, lecturer, curator, docent, even a renowned collector.

The key is to select your area of collecting with care. Too often people begin by collecting some exotic foreign stuff because of what turns out to be a passing fascination or because of a fadish trend that is currently the craze. It makes more sense to look at your home, your leisure-time pursuits, your collections of jewelry. Discover what you already collect. Perhaps it might be fine china, rifles, books on the sea, stamps, clocks, or antiques. The point: Know to a certainty that your interest in them will not pass overnight to another fadish craze, one that requires a separate expertise.

This fascination with your collection is mandatory

because the world of your collection—journals, associations, shows, museums, to name four examples—may become a large part of your life. Your study should include history, design, the likelihood of forgeries, comparative values, the craftsmen of different periods. Eventually you'll see the $750 item that's for sale at $350 and know that it's a buy. You'll be able to pay $250 for an item that's worth $1,000 but has not sold because no one has authenticated it. You'll see the Tiffany signature and know it can't be a Tiffany. Restorations and reproductions have value, which could create an advantage. You'll know who prospective buyers are because you'll be competing with them for certain items.

All of this, of course, takes time. Most books dealing with collectibles have much to say about *caveat emptor* —buyer beware. That's sound advice, but it doesn't go far enough. The process described here should give you the advantage where your knowledge is superior to the person with whom you negotiate. The best advice is not to plunge until you gain expertise; start small and trade upwards on your profits. This book will discuss how to select good and reputable dealers, how to spot the flim-flam artist, the faked items, the forgeries, where to go for advice, appraisals, and authentications—and when.

Inevitably, in any quest for information there are one or two conversations that bring together all of the threads of information. As I talked and corresponded with these experts two things became strikingly clear. First, most of the appraisers-collectors enjoy themselves immensely, and, secondly, they make comfortable livings. Not a bad combination. And, significantly, these people keep saying that there are not nearly enough experts, whether they be dealers, appraisers, or authors of price guides or investing guides. In fact, the American Society of Appraisers (ASA), the leading force in a building national drive to put some kind of legitimacy and licensing of appraisers in collectibles, has but 150 personal property appraisers. That's for all of the country.

One of them, William Lutton of San Francisco, a

leading authority on French antique furniture, was talking of his experiences when suddenly the process or manner in which a collector should proceed came clear. Lutton's thoughts and insights are valuable because he has turned his love of the graceful, fragile, yet sturdy French antiques into a fine way of life. He lives in a spacious condominium that embraces one floor of one of San Francisco's Pacific Heights highrise buildings. The furniture, paintings, and tapestries in his home are lovely and exquisite, but at the same time warm and inviting. "When people buy furniture," he says, "it should be with the idea of using it. Profit follows pleasure.

"I'm really concerned to see young people buy paintings and furniture at outrageous sums, particularly when they don't really like it. They buy it because an interior decorator or some friend says it is right. If you try to collect for a profit, that determines your taste, which means it can't be that enjoyable a pursuit.

"I think there are four rules. First, a person must enjoy the time necessary to find the right pieces. Second, the pieces must be usable. There's nothing worse than walking into a home that has rooms of furniture that are never used. Third, the pieces must grow on the collector. Go back to a shop as often as possible to look them over before buying. The dealers will probably think you're casing the joint but that's all right. Finally, the piece must be relaxing and a pleasure to the eye. Too many times a piece turns out to be sterile. Most times that comes from using one dealer or a decorator in hurry-up-and-be-done-with-it efforts. There's little enjoyment or intellectual satisfaction when you haven't participated in the hunt yourself and when you don't know what you're sitting on, looking at, or oohing and aahing about."

The affable appraiser, who lectures on his speciality at Stanford University, says the search can take months and years. "You should go to all the best places—the shops, the museums. Learn what you like. Learn all you can and then finally go out and try to find the steal. It can take years to accumulate a house of fine antiques—

you need all the help you can get from friends, dealers, and relatives. It can be exciting when you start finding what you want. I was in a shop in Los Altos and found four Chinese scrolls (each hangs with the rich appearance of a fine tapestry). I talked the guy into selling them for $20 each. They're worth $4,000 in all."

The key is to have enough interest in collecting items like French antiques so that expertise is acquired. "Ideally the person should read not only about the furniture and the craftsmen who created the pieces, but also about the social, political, and economic factors that dictated the furniture be made in that style. It is much harder to get stung then because if it is advertised as being of a certain period, you'll know if it is of a representative style. Still, we all get caught. I bought a long French Regency bench that was beautifully hand carved. I was sure that I at least had a fine reproduction. After I got home I discovered a very small 'made in Italy' on the underside. But I really like the piece itself so I feel I received value for my money."

Lutton is a perfect example of a man who loves the beauty and grace of the pieces with which he routinely works. He says that he still learns things everyday. There's probably no other investment or speculation where an individual has so much ready reference material and where its use can have such an immediate application. The old dictum truly holds: the greater the effort, the greater the reward.

The view of the experts is that few dealers, most of whom are not highly specialized in their knowledge, can be rated as expert. So when a collector gains a true understanding of his field, he also gains an advantage in many situations. More on this later, but nearly all appraisers/dealers describe how a collector should operate in a highly similar way.

Tim Morrow, an appraiser of Oriental art, jade, and pearls in Lahaina, Hawaii, succinctly explains, "Browse in museums; talk to curators; go to dealers and handle as many pieces that look similar; ask a million questions; try to deal with a reliable individual whenever possible. Try to 'grade up' by trading off mistakes for fewer but better pieces as one becomes educated in a special area of collecting."

Later chapters will deal in detail with many of the following guidelines for successful collecting, but a summary here will best explain the kind of in-depth effort and practices a collector should adopt. It must be understood that no single one of the experts recommends all of these suggestions, but that the list is a distillation of the advice they offer.

1. Confine your collecting to as narrow a field as you can. If you select rare books, limit your purchases to a category such as military history and to only the best and rarest affordable. For example, the battles of the Civil War within Kansas. Or you might collect signed, first edition Hemingways, Steinbecks, or Gertrude Steins. If the collector starts with a well-defined collection, he stands a superior chance of becoming knowledgeable in a reasonable time, and consequently, a collector who is finding both profit and pleasure.

2. Read, research, and study. A collector of French antique furniture must not only know who the craftsmen were, but also what they made, and which pieces are likely to be authentic. He should also know the social conditions that created the pieces, how highly they were prized then and by which class—the merchants, peasants, or nobility. Art history is an honorable pursuit taught at the finest universities; likewise, so is the history of antique furniture, classic automobiles, books, swords . . . .

3. Knowledge equals profit. F. Herbert Hoover, a grandson of the late president, says one of his great thrills came through his "eye" and his knowledge of the work of Thomas Hart Benton. In a small shop he found a lithograph and recognized it as an original; for a couple of dollars he purchased a work worth hundreds of dollars. Most collectors would be satisfied with knowing that their purchases are made at fair market prices, at least initially. But knowledge also means the collector may become in demand as an appraiser and author . . .

this field is growing and the people who know are doing quite well.

4. Handle the merchandise. Only through examining fine items, developing their aura and touch, studying them, can a person gain that sixth sense that screams: Authentic, buy, cherish, own! Auction houses are usually operated in a manner to give the bidders a day or two—at least the morning of the auction—to examine and determine value of items. Once dealers recognize a collector as more than a gadfly, they understand the mission of his repeated calls. Frequent museums, exhibitions, shows, association meetings.

5. Get immersed in the hunt. Q. David Bowers, the popular author on rare coins and a respected Los Angeles auctioneer, flatly states that a collector should spend 10 per cent of his money on gathering information and knowledge. Ask dealers to call you when certain items surface, seek out the remote shops, go to "garage" or house sales, auctions.

6. Expect authentication or documentation that the item to be bought is precisely what it is represented to be. The most reputable dealers stand firmly behind their wares, offering to make the buyer whole if the item is ever found to be other than what the dealer said it was. Most expensive pieces carry a provenance, a history of the piece that shows who has owned it and any repairs or restorations. A provenance can be established for a piece. But appraiser fees and calls to other dealers are necessary to compile the needed folio. Undocumented items at auctions can be especially risky buys.

7. Use an appraiser or friendly dealer whenever you are in doubt as to value and authenticity. Fees vary, depending upon the amount of time and effort needed by an appraiser. That will be dealt with fully later.

8. Buy only what you can afford, comfortably. The collector should let the size of early purchases reflect his level of knowledge. Gems, coins, and other pieces have ready markets, but often the collector will find that selling at the right price will determine whether he profits from his effort. Patience is absolutely essen-

tial. With some expensive pieces, it may take months or years to find the buyer who understands the righteousness of your asking price.

9. Purchase nothing that does not please and excite you greatly. If a piece is to be in your collection or home for months while the right buyer takes his time finding the item, it should be a joy to possess. More important, if the collector does not love or enjoy his collection, he will hardly spend the effort to increase his knowledge and the value of his collection.

10. Seek out and patronize the best and most reputable dealers. These people can minimize early mistakes and lead the beginning collector down a path that will bring pleasure and not the pain that comes from bad buys. They stand behind their merchandise, and they will inform you when an item you seek is available. Many experts agree that a person can go to many dealers and say, "I've so much money to spend and I want to build a collection. What do I do?" "We love those people," says James Willis, who operates an African art and sculpture gallery in San Francisco. "I find myself often selling that client a piece for a few hundred dollars less because I know it is all that he can afford. But I also know that if he has a valuable and profitable collection and believes in me, we'll do much more business in the future."

11. Go to the auctions. Increasingly these days, that's where the action is greatest. But remember the competition there includes dealers and decorators and appraisers, all of whom are professionals and undoubtedly understand something of the value of the pieces they wish to purchase. Here, *caveat emptor* is really necessary. Don't get caught up in the mood of the place and go after pieces on impulse. Establish what the piece is worth to you ahead of time.

12. Trade up. Use profits to seek out the better and more expensive items. A work of art or an antique that was common and poorly made will very nearly always remain common. Roman coins, of which there are still many, can still be bought for a pittance. The rare item

of extraordinary condition was highly prized when created and will remain a cherished collectors' item. A collector should strive for the "best of the rare."

13. Beware of fakes and forgeries. With the increasing number of dealers, many of them hardly know more than most collectors. They can and do make honest mistakes. Remember that glass is easily copied and that signatures can be added to most pieces, whether furniture, glass, or books. Phoney documents are far easier to produce than faked or forged pieces.

14. And then there's the flim flam artist. They gravitate to money and action. If coins are hot, these folks will be in that market. Motel room showings might be their arena, or cut-rate offers in periodicals. Most publishers attempt to check out their advertisers, but they, like buyers, usually learn too late if an advertiser is less than he advertises. Don't, for example, buy paintings or lithographs framed under glass, without inspecting them.

15. Join clubs and associations. People with your own interests will be good friends, comrades, and sources of information that will help build a fine collection. Subscribe to trade journals and periodicals. They are fine sources of data and many offer good places to advertise the pieces you wish to sell.

Time, yes, it takes time. But the time the collector spends reading and perusing and browsing is much like the time the stock market trader spends poring over the tape, charting the movement of the averages, studying earnings reports. But the collector can know he is becoming an expert with a real chance to turn profits when he finds, suddenly, that he knows more of his specialized area of collecting than dealers who tend to be generalized.

The collector then has the advantage, the knowledge. Finally he can begin moving into larger purchases, trading up to the rare pieces. It's essential to possess that strong desire to own the best. This is what many married couples do as they move from home to home over the years, each time trading up to a more expensive home in a better neighborhood or suburb.

Buying and selling are complex arts and each requires thought and the help of the more expert collectors, dealers, and appraisers. Generally, the collector buys and sells in the same manner and through the same channels. Expect to spend as much time selling an item as it initially took to find and buy it. The most common markets are, naturally enough, the dealers. They possessed 90 per cent of the volume before World War II, but today many experts say auction houses now handle fully 50 per cent of the action. Too, there are the shows and flea markets, advertisements in trade publications. It's wise to become familiar with how each of these outlets works.

Perhaps here's the right place to raise again the flag of caution. *Caveat emptor*—buyer beware. Not all collector-investors, even the accomplished ones, make money. There are notable examples, such as Eli "Grandpa" Springs who was a respected collector. During the 1920s he frequented the gilded auction houses in New York City and amassed a huge collection that is estimated to have cost him about $700,000. After his death in 1934, his collection was sold for less than one-third of his investment. Ah, yes, the Depression. But it was not a uniformly grim time for collectors, and few of them took the bath of the stock market eagles.

Collecting can become a mania. What now seems like hilarious advice—and probably was a bit of tongue in cheek even at the turn of the century—was written by Jules Fleury-Husson, a Parisian who used the pseudonym, Champfleury. His book, *Les Petits Mysteres de L'Hotel des Ventes,* included 60 hints to auction goers. Wesley Towner quotes some of them in his book, *The Elegant Auctioneers:*

"A plain overcoat without furs or trimmings is the dress most propitious for making a good strike . . . To let yourself be carried away by the tide of bidding is to expect to make your fortune at roulette . . . Fortify your nerves by washing in cold water every morning . . . Don't irritate your stomach by spicy meals . . . A bar of chocolate, or anything sweet, fortifies the system around four o'clock, when the bidding gets hot . . . A bottle of smelling salts is indispensable to combat the exhalations of the crowd . . . Marriage and collecting, two natural rivals, together make life unbearable . . . Collectors who marry should abdicate and sell their accumulations . . . Every collection that does not offer a panorama ceaselessly renewed palls, like a too faithful wife . . . All irrelevant thought has to be sacrificed to the collection. Do not occupy yourself with politics; never go to the theater; forbid yourself to open a book; scorn the pleasures of family; always have ready money in your pocket; arrive each day at the auction rooms at one o'clock, leave at six, return for the evening sales. With this you will have a full life. You will be a perfect collector."

Indeed.

Collecting involves much more than a mere hunt for items to be accumulated. It is not easy for the collector to shift fields for though he knows the process of buying and dealing, he loses his advantageous edge of superior knowledge. And in today's world the possessions a person accumulates, his collection, reflect much of his nature. Perhaps this explains why mechanics or race drivers own classic machines, housewives collect rare plates, authors delight in first editions by great writers.

Just as important, when a collector becomes an authority, he will suddenly find other people seeking him out for advice, authentications, appraisals, lectures, periodical articles, donations to exhibits, participation in organizations. His collection becomes very much an integral part of his life, and it dictates, to a great extent, his friends, cohorts, and leisure-time activities.

John Bedford writes in *The Collecting Man,* "At some point the collector finds he is an authority and knows more than most general dealers. A number of things happen to the collector, he becomes an archaeologist, historian, anthropologist, connoisseur of art—he will know why furniture was of a certain style in one era and another style in another . . . (and) he has made a corner in something of interest to the rest of us. What we want during his lifetime is descriptive chapter and verse, not only about the collection itself, but on the way he collected it and what he learnt in the process. We want him to document finds, telling us where and in what circumstances he found them. In the fields of ethnographica and archaeology, devastating harm has been done to the cause of scientific and social history by thoughtless and indiscriminate looting and excavating, destroying forever much data and robbing posterity of vital knowledge. When (he) finds a thing lying in a place where it has been undisturbed for centuries, it is his duty to his fellow man to record the place and the date and the circumstances of the find."

There are, of course, levels of collecting. The collector must determine his goal in accumulating his collection. It might be to amass capital, to beat inflation, to surround himself with objects of great pleasure and joy, to gain status and renown, and, even, to shield his assets from the tax gatherer. Next, he must determine the destiny of his collection. Will he leave it for a thoughtless relative to place on the block in an estate sale? As tax problems for his children? Donation to a museum? Funds to live a comfortable retirement? The original stock for his own dealership, his own shop where he can easily pass on his knowledge and experience?

These are weighty matters that are best left in the back of the mind until the proper course becomes abundantly clear. Yet collections proved of immense value to many Europeans fleeing the Nazi advance. Many stuffed suitcases with jewels, paintings, stamps, and objets d'art and fled with a fortune in their hands. Hoover says he knows a collector who has spent his life always trading up for better paintings. "But each of his newly purchased masterpieces is smaller than the one he sold or traded in. He is down to using a very small suitcase for their storage."

But another man who recently died in San Diego left his children, who now have their own family, with tremendous problems. "My dad was an inveterate collector. He bought old movie cameras out of Hollywood that were used in the days of the silent pictures. He has a fine firearm collection. There are beautiful pieces of antique furniture. Much of it is of value, but I really don't know about any of it except for the firearm collection," his son says. "Now my brother and I have to go through every room of this huge house. It would have been much simpler for my father, who knew about his collections, to have made provisions for them after his death."

In the past year or two, with gold bullion not proving to be the solid hedge against inflation and recession, more and more people have been moving heavily into collectibles. Banks, to these people, are suspect because they might fail. "The rarity of collectors' items gives a value to an item that bullion does not possess," says Bowers. "Bullion is a commodity, a purely speculative venture."

But more on the investment versus speculation considerations and the track records of collectibles in the next chapter. Men such as Joseph Hirshhorn and Norton Simon have become richer because of their collections, and they carry out the axiom that the best and most successful collectors are those who collect out of the joy of the hunt, the love of antiquity, the beauty of the pieces. Some have learned that in areas like furniture that some reproductions produced about a hundred years after our founding Colonial period have a greater quality of craftsmanship than the originals. But to them, the craftsmen of both periods become personalities and to locate a particular hero's work is indeed an emotional lift.

There are fads, trends, and crazes—some bubbling up one year and bursting the next. But through it all, if the collector knows more than the dealer or rival collector he buys and sells from, he'll spot the price movements earlier. He'll know that quality is always in demand and there is, to be sure, comfort in that knowledge.

Finding Future Values

"For the purchase of any collectible to be considered an investment," says Frank Knight, editor-publisher of the *Collectors' Weekly,* "the collectible must have an established track record."

It would be a fine thing to lay out guidelines for investing, for speculating, or to define the comfortable middle-ground between the two. But any market for collectibles can move dramatically at times, and it's usually as fickle as a painted lady. While one period of antique furniture might be soaring in price on the West Coast, another might be increasing on the eastern seaboard. In fact, the section of the country has much to do with the different levels of popularity for the same works of art. It is knowing what direction prices are moving, what is hugely popular and where, and what might become the next national craze—such as the nostalgia boom—that can spell the difference between routine and profitable collecting.

Since World War II, prices for nearly all collectibles have continually moved ahead, though prices have dipped for short periods of time. Each collector must decide for himself what constitutes a track record and whether his purchase is an investment to be cherished or a speculation to be held only until a profit appears. For example, there's good data on what has happened to the rare-coin market since the middle 1930s, but is that a long enough duration to know with confidence how the coins might fare in the differing economic climes of the future? Most coin experts would argue it is.

A comparison of "compound annual rates of return" from different types of investments prepared by the Commodity Investors Research Group in Los Angeles gives what is a terribly flattering—though well documented—look at rare coins as an investment:

Compound Annual Rates of Return

Investment Type	1947-1973	1969-1973	1973
Rare U.S. Coins	19.0%	27.3%	160.0%
Standard and Poor's 500 Stock Composite (Capital Appreciation + Dividend Yield)	10.7%	2.3%	-23.1%
Dow Jones Industrial Average (Capital Appreciation + Dividend Yield)	9.9%	3.2%	-16.0%
Standard and Poor's "AAA" Industrial Bonds	7.8%	8.9%	8.7%
Municipal Bonds	5.7%	5.9%	5.2%
Rural Real Estate	5.6%	7.3%	——
Silver Bullion	4.4%	10.5%	61.6%
Gold Bullion	3.5%	21.6%	72.3%
Foreign Currency	1.08%	3.9%	7.6%

Let's stick to coins to see how a hobby could become an investment vehicle. Q. David Bowers, one of the most authoritative writers on rare coins today and a Los Angeles rare coin auctioneer, contends that coin values will increase if the number of collectors increases. "A rare coin is like a rare painting in that its value is based on an increased demand for it in the future, and today, more and more people are finding increased leisure to pursue hobbies." He says that during the Depression there were only a few thousand coin collectors in this country and that though values dropped for a couple of years, there was "a boom in 1934-1935 and growing interest through the decade."

That interest never diminished. In 1946 the first *Guidebook of U.S. Coins* was published; since then more than 10 million copies have been sold, which makes it one of the top ten best-selling books in U.S. history. Bowers says that an investment of $1,000 in quality rare coins in 1948 would have been worth more than $30,000 in 1974. "We've never had a client who has held onto his coins for a few years lose money," he says.

"In fact, I've helped many of them become millionaires."

Bowers contrasts rare coins with gold bullion. "Coins are a fine investment with calculated risks. Gold and silver bullion are true speculations." He adds that coins generally are not subject to property tax, only capital gains tax when sold.

Another expert on coins, Frank Knight, says, "There are always hills and valleys in a chart of price movements of rare coins, but each time the valley is higher than before." He counsels that a person should become a collector, "an astute collector," before becoming an investor. "Knowledge is value in collecting," he adds. "You have protections in the stock market that you never get in collectibles."

The coin market did not remain firm during 1975. Franz Pick wrote in *Barron's* in January 1976, "After booming in 1974, with gains of up to 100 per cent, numismatic coins took a tumble last year. The average decline was around 60 per cent. Nonetheless, some items fetched good prices at U.S. auctions. For example, an 1838 Proof U.S. Gold Eagle coin topped the list at $105,000—for just 15 grams of fine gold worth about $70. An 1828 Half Eagle ($5 face value) was bid up to $92,500." The finest and rarest coins held their value best, yet experts point out that most coins are still well above 1973 values.

Investing in collectibles, then, has many pitfalls quite similar to the stock market. Timing is essential. And in each field the experts often tie booms into national fads and crazes. Take the interest in nostalgia items, and in the celebration of the nation's bicentennial. Many collectors have been buying in anticipation of increasing values for years.

There are no generalizations that really hold true regarding price movements in collectibles. Sure, nearly everything is much dearer today than 20 years ago, and often dramatically more so. But the collector has to know and study his field, perhaps charting price movements just as stock traders chart the stock averages in their daily fluctuations. If an item has been appreciating in value for the past five years and suddenly brings somewhat less at auction, it might be time to consider selling a collection of similar items.

Undoubtedly, nearly any serious collector who has been accumulating items for several years has shown a profit—and a sizeable one. But before becoming too enthusiastic, look at the "track record" of paintings and rare books. Prices of Renoirs and Rembrandts bring millions at auction houses and even our contemporary giants like Andy Warhol and Rauschenberg command prices in excess of $100,000. Yet Gerald Reitlinger, the author of the painstakingly researched and highly respected three-volume work, *The Economics of Taste,* says "art as an investment is a conception scarcely older than the early 1950s."

Reitlinger's view is unsettling to the investor in art, and it is a well-documented opinion that should be taken seriously. "The real peak of the art market was somewhere about 1912. Works of art which became established in the course of the past century as the highest achievements of their kind, have often failed to maintain the level of 1912 in real money terms and sometimes they have failed to maintain it even in paper figures (that reflect the ravages of inflation). Rembrandt himself with no less than 14 six-figure prices in the course of the 1960s will be seen to have done little more than stay abreast of inflation in the light of some of the prices which were paid before the depression of the 1930s."

He talks of entire schools of painters whose "names created salesrooms epics in their day (the 19th century) while their decline in the present century contains the ingredients of high drama . . . Their present situation is at least a reminder that not all art-hoarding has been an investment." He decries those brokers who push art as an investment. "Theirs is the simple creed that, while the good need not be expensive, the expensive must always be good . . ."

"Enormous profits," he allows, have been made in the past two decades by those who follow the fashionable trends. He terms this speculation. "The only investors were those who never meant to invest at all." He means the buyers who purchased merely for pleasure, aesthetic pleasure. He chronicles this century, citing the peak in 1912, how the price of nearly everything plummeted in the 1930s, and how nearly everything soared in the 1960s. "The lesser slump of 1968-69 produced a paradox which threatened to become an orthodoxy. It is that works of art go up in proportion as capital values, profits and dividends decline, that as substitutes for money, works of art are not liable to the same erosions as money itself."

History does not bear this out, of course. The investing market in collectibles was as jumbled in 1975 as the rest of the economy. French Impressionistic paintings jumped in value by more than 200 per cent, watercolors of great masters increased by about 125 per cent, antique silver increased in value by 45 per cent for the second straight year, Oriental paintings increased by about 95 per cent.

On the down side, clocks, watches, violins, and stringed instruments decreased by about 30 per cent, but that came after four years of rising prices for these works of art. Generally, prices paid for paintings by the great masters were off considerably, and prices for antique American furniture, after years of rising prices and a 200 per cent increase in 1974, finally fell to about half of those heights.

Rare books make an interesting story. In 1975 the price of them increased about 85 per cent, but generally they still do not command the prices—in real money terms—that they did earlier this century. They were the collectibles of the very rich about 1900. The first Gutenburg Bible was bought in this country in 1847 for $2,500, it sold in 1897 for $20,000, and in 1911 Henry Huntington paid $50,000 for it. In 1926 the Mellon copy of the Gutenburg sold for $106,000. Though a copy of the Bay Psalm Book—the first book printed in the Anglo-American colonies in 1640—brought $151,000 in 1947, the 1920s were—and still are—the high-water mark of the "bibliomania" fever.

Very few books have equaled those prices since then. However, for the past 15 years rare books and manuscripts have been increasing in value by about 25 to 30 per cent annually. Fiction has never been as highly prized by collectors, and the most highly esteemed collections these days specialize in geographical history, such as works on California and Texas. One reason prices have climbed to huge figures is that most of the truly rare books are now held by institutions and museums. But some works of fiction, for example, may still offer great rewards to the collector. A set of autographed first editions by Mark Twain has been offered at $1,500, and signed Hemingways and Steinbecks can be purchased for about $25.

Enough of this rarefied atmosphere of the truly dear items. Perhaps the greatest explosion of interest has been in once-common items such as bottles, comic books, and farm implements, though some older items related to the railroads are becoming quite expensive. A person may collect them because of a fascination for them, even though many have little intrinsic value. They become fads, crazes, and the market for them may drop as rapidly as it spurts. But it is in spotting the new craze early that big money can be made—and quickly.

Phil Moran, an appraiser-dealer in antique furniture, objets d'art, and other fine collectibles in San Antonio, explains how he and his wife, a respected appraiser-dealer herself, foresaw the boom in Depression glass. "We had seen so many other items become instant collectibles," he says, "and we knew there was a lot of this glass around. That's one of the prerequisites. The nostalgia boom was building and many items dating from the Depression were catching on. So we started buying Depression glass for a nickel and a dime a piece. We had our friends, other dealers scouting around for us. I suspect we collected about 18,000 pieces." Many of those nickel-dime variety pieces have climbed to where they sell for $5 to $15 a piece. "We became very confident as we collected," he adds. "We sold our stocks and invested in the glass. Sure, it was a speculation, but we figured that it was an area of expertise at which we had a better chance than other folks." And did they ever.

There's conflicting evidence about just how well the average collector does financially, but most of the really grim tales have to do with those who are taken in by the "instant collectibles" offered through the mails. Those mass-marketed, supposedly limited-edition medallions, coins, plates, and books are heavily advertised and promoted as "great opportunities." One was a collection of expensively and beautifully bound great books offered to American Express cardholders. The offering didn't even list which of the great books would be among the titles of the collection. Still, that offering sold $90 million worth, which means "limited" was defined by how many people were willing to cough up the bucks.

Seymour Freeman, an appraiser-dealer in gems and jewelry in Scottsdale, Arizona, says the mail-order offerings on gems such as uncut diamonds work much the same way. "I've checked out those offerings," he says, "and they seem to be about 20 per cent above market value."

Alex Sabbadini, an auctioneer-appraiser in Sacramento, says an influx of young collectors is adding to the market's boom. "Years ago a young man would come in and say, 'My family left me a housefull of old stuff, mostly junk. Can you take it off my hands?' He didn't know or care about antiques. Most of them didn't appreciate what their grandparents had acquired. But now you find these same young people among the most enthusiastic antique nuts. They realize they'll have no problem getting their money back out of their stuff if they have to move. There's a great difference between their buying a Victorian table lamp for $150 and selling it a couple of years later for $200 and buying a chic, modern Swedish lamp for $100 and selling it two years later for $20."

This kind of buying is a good introduction to value

for it explains many of the complex factors that make values fluctuate. Most experts tell collectors to concentrate on learning quality and taste first, figuring that if the less-than-professional buyer purchases items with intrinsic worth he stands less chance of being badly burned. It is true that the best of the rare normally appreciates more than the common items in value, but it is also true that the fast money is made by hopping in ahead of the beginning of a craze.

The differences between those two types of buying may well define the limits of speculating and investing. The investment has a track record, usually an object with an allure based on superb craftsmanship or inspiring genius. It may represent classic good taste, and it nearly always is pointed to as possessing quality. If the market for any collectible continues to increase, the best of the rare will lead the advance of prices. For example, consider the 15 known 1804 silver dollars. In 1970 one sold for $77,500; in 1972, for $100,000; in 1973, for $150,000; and in 1974, for $165,000. The risk of owning an 1804 silver dollar is not great, understandably.

Speculating is another game. Here, the collector hopes to buy items that have not yet gained great value, or at least have not gained much of the huge value that the collector foresees. Remember Phil Moran's plunge into Depression glass. Other examples are the huge price increases in aged wood-burning stoves, pushed even higher by the energy crunch, the nostalgia boom, and the return to nature by many younger people. Snuff boxes, too, skyrocketed in the past few years, many increasing in value by 10 times.

It is difficult to spot coming trends and fads. "There's a pretty good demand for nearly anything collectible, except for things produced in the past 10 to 20 years," says Sabbadini. Yet appraisers see new fads developing. Among their favorite would-be bargains at today's prices:

In collectibles: all elements of the railway industry dated before 1930, new Tiffany-type art glass by contemporary artists, photographica, antique silver, desk and table items in bronze or sterling made in the first quarter of this century, American pottery and red ware in ceramics, Galle and Navajo rugs, automated instruments like pianos, archestrions, and juke boxes.

In edged weapons: everything from pocket knives to broad swords.

In coins: rare and semi-rare U.S. and foreign gold and nearly any foreign coin, even minor varieties.

In stringed instruments; the violin.

In objets d'Art: cloisonne, Chinese glass, high-grade porcelain figures in fine limited editions, Japanese byoubu screens and other items used by old artists such as suzuri bacos, brush holders, brush washers, and brush rests.

In philately: stamps associated with postal history.

In rugs: Any authentic Persian or Oriental rug.

In fine arts: from Islamic countries and Persia in particular, Oceania, the Orient, and Africa.

In paintings: by German expressionists, contemporary Americans, and Old Masters by lesser-known artists.

Speculation isn't for everyone. Listing what might be the current and coming crazes is a bit like the scene out of the movie, *The Graduate*. Dustin Hoffman had returned home from school and at a party that his parents threw for him, one middle-aged man cornered him and told him he was going to, in effect, give him the secret to success. The man whispered, conspiratorially, "plastics." Information, after all, is useless without knowledge, insight, and a way of putting the information to work.

So these pointers toward what might become hot collectible items should be viewed as just that, though they come from the group of people who might be in closest touch with these markets. These experts also provide data about crazes that seem to have run their courses. They say collectibles of these types probably are peaking or have peaked in value and now are sliding back in value. Again, that may be true for most pieces, but there are always works of art that retain value because of their beauty and timeless grace.

The experts in all areas of collecting, particularly the dealers and appraisers, keep close tabs on market movements. They contend the best dealers make their best gains when they properly interpret the market—before the trend or change attracts the eye of most of their competition. If these experts are right, now is the time to sell items in these categories, unless, of course, the item is of unusual value, rarity, or possesses a greater significance in the collection. Admittedly, these areas or categories of items are broad, but generally the market moves broadly in collectibles.

These are the items that authorities believe have peaked in price: Tiffany items, the pop artists of the 1960s, French Impressionistic paintings and graphics, high grade turquoise, aquamarine, pottery and basketry, fine French furniture, Art Deco items, Greek and Roman art, firearms of the American Civil War, oak furniture circa 1900, collectors' bottles, Indian jewelry, and gold, particularly common U.S. double eagles.

There may be some overlap between those items that supposedly were peaking in price and these items that are considered to be the "current craze," and there may be a similar overlap between the current craze and what these experts believe will be the next craze. Still, much can be gleaned. It might mean the market remains strong though many collectors and dealers are losing faith in the item's continued demand, continued upward movement in price. If, however, the item is considered to be currently popular and also considered to be one of the coming "hot" items, now could be a grand time to move into the market.

These are, of course, but guidelines and the general observations of the market by experts. Too, the collector must understand the way of the book publishers; there is always a time lag that makes information like this some months old, which does not detract from its value but should, nonetheless, be considered.

The current craze:

In firearms: World War I and II handguns and especially German Lugers, American Revolutionary War weapons, Colt and Smith & Wesson handguns, 1850 to present.

In coins: U.S. type coins, foreign crown-size coins.

In collectibles: art glass, antique jewelry, Art Deco items, items of early American heritage (the bloom lingers from the Bicentennial), Depression glass, tin types, fruit jars, finest quality plates, turquoise jewelry, leaded glass lampshades.

In stringed instruments: the Viola Da Gamba.

In furniture: oak (circa 1900-1920), and Victoriana (1830-1900).

In objets d'art: netsuke, fine lacquer ware, snuff bottles, fine stone carvings, old and fine ivory carvings (many recent reproductions of these to be wary of), 17th Century pottery, Orientalia.

In paintings: Andy Warhol and giants of the school, and contemporary in general.

In philately, plate-number blocks and stamps in coils.

Speculation is not the best nor the easiest way of making immediate profits. The never-fail method is to learn your area of collecting so thoroughly that dealers will possess no advantage over you, so that in fact you'll possess that advantage, which will enable you to negotiate prices from superior knowledge. Then, when a table is offered at $350, because no one has yet documented its authenticity, you, the collector, can purchase that $1,100 table because you know its value. Don't tell that dealer he just took a whipping, however, because you might want to do business with him again.

Many times values can be greatly enhanced if the collector goes to the trouble—indeed, fun—of gathering the provenance for a work of art himself. About a year ago, for example, a number of Picasso graphics, purportedly signed in pencil by the artist, arrived in San Francisco. The importer of the lithographs assured me they were authentic, but he said he had no documentation. Still, they were priced at $40 each, which means they were a steal if they were indeed signed by Picasso. I knew, though, that once they were irrefutably Picassos the price of them would climb. I purchased two of them and proceeded to work at compiling a provenance myself. Just as important, I liked the graphics immensely and would not have been too disappointed or hurt if I later learned they could not be established as Picassos.

First, I persuaded the San Francisco gallery owner to give me photocopies of his bill of sale from the Paris gallery, which is one of the galleries known to handle the artist's work. I had the San Francisco dealer authenticate my copies as parts of the consignment that he had received from Paris. I could have written the Paris gallery but it didn't prove necessary. Next, I procured an appraisal from the curator of a San Francisco gallery that deals in Picassos, then another opinion from another gallery curator that the lithographs were authentic, and finally another appraisal. Today, I still own the graphics but I—and the experts—am convinced that their value is worth between $600 and $850, rather than the $40 I paid for them. In this instance a speculation became an investment. But as I said, I haven't attempted to sell them so it's not wise to crow about profits before they're realized.

Rules abound regarding the use of money for speculation and investment. Nearly all experts repeatedly counsel against borrowing money to build a collection, just as they counsel against buying anything you don't like, even if it might be at a good price. Too, they always say that the collection should be the finest work affordable, rather than two lesser items. Always question the dealer or other party why he isn't selling the item at full price if it is such a solid value. The prospect is that a collector might end up with worthless objects, which are not pleasing to him and for which there is no buyer.

Undeniably, fortunes have been made, are being made, and will be made in collecting. But just as surely collectors have lost money and will lose money on their collections. The best safeguard for any collector is to demand papers proving the authenticity of any purchase, and for the collector to purchase from dealers who will guarantee the work of art is what it is represented to be. If not, the buyer is to be made whole for his purchase. And do not be so niggardly in your purchasing that an appraiser is considered too great an expense; it is the document the appraiser gives you that helps create the full value of your purchase.

But start slowly, concerning yourself at first with gaining knowledge both about the field in which you are collecting and with how to properly buy and sell. The alternative to expending such effort is to find a person who is both trustworthy and fully qualified to invest your money. Some groups of physicians have been using dealers to purchase rare-coin collections for years. Their fund has increased greatly in value and they possess that smug look of doctors who, for once, properly diagnosed the condition of the economy. You too can choose dealers or other experts to help build a collection. In some instances, this may be the only way the collector can cut through the tremendous markups dealers place on merchandise.

Dealing With Dealers

The wife of a backwoods lawyer in California's historic gold-rush country opened her "antique" shop in early 1976. "I've always loved the beauty of many of the fine old pieces," she says, "and I've spent years browsing through shops, buying for our home, for friends and relatives, and talking to an awful lot of antique dealers. I know I'm not really an expert, but there are some things I know a great deal about—like brass beds, chairs, clocks, and stained glass. I'll just try to add on a fair markup to make the shop pay its way. It's simply something I've always wanted to do. It'll be fun."

She's hardly unusual. The number of antique or yesteryear shop dealers has doubled since 1970, and many of these dealers are avid collectors who saw their collections getting too large. They decided the best way to market their collections would be to open a shop. Most of these dealers are honest, but most of them aren't expertly informed in a broad range of collectibles.

This tells the collector a few things. First, there are bargains to be bought from these dealers, if the collector knows more about an item or work of art than the dealer. Second, the dealer has not been in business long enough to establish a well-founded reputation and, it just might be, won't be in business for too many years. It does little good to get certain guarantees from a dealer if you can't depend upon the dealer remaining in business to stand behind his word.

But even the established dealers hold different views as to what their obligation to the buyer is. There are many, of course, who are to be implicitly trusted and valued. Finding a dealer of that stature can be one of the collector's most important actions. Then, there are dealers to be avoided, either because their information is bad, they simply don't know, or they participate in shady or fraudulent practices. A dealer can be as wrong about an item's value as the prospective buyer, though the dealer might not admit it.

The best dealers can be recognized by the way they operate. They know their merchandise, but if they are not entirely certain whether a work of art is truly a masterpiece, they will not represent it as an extremely valuable example of the artist's work. What happens in the event the dealer does represent an item, a book, for example, as possessing great value—and then weeks or months later the buyer learns the book is not what the dealer represented it to be? Warren Howell, the internationally respected dealer in San Francisco, allows that the situation does occur.

He tells of the time his client had paid nearly $100,000 for a rare book, which later proved to be less than what Howell represented it to be. "I credited him with $100,000," says Howell. The dealer was fortunate that the collector was a longstanding client of Howell's, yet this guarantee that the book or work of art is in fact what it is represented to be is the collector's greatest protection. A dealer of Howell's stature seldom makes major mistakes, but it is significant that when it did occur he stood behind his representation of value. It is a quality to be highly prized, and a quality that the collector should seek out in dealers.

Other dealers operate at the other end of the spectrum. One New York City antique dealer sold a beautifully fragile chair to a customer for $8,000. He had represented the chair to be an $8,000 antique, but an appraiser later found that the dealer had manufactured the chair himself at a cost of about $350.

The experts say few dealers know as much as they should and certainly not as much as most collectors believe they do. Still, there are ways to get a dealer working for the collector and even better ways to check on a dealer's integrity. Despite the closer definitions of a dealer's responsibilities that are developing because of the consumer movement, the buyer is still very much on his own and it's still very much a *caveat emptor* situation. But with a sensible and knowledgeable approach to buying, the collector builds in great safeguards for himself.

A dealer should be prepared to offer a provenance, particularly for expensive items. The provenance amounts to documentation that might trace the history of the work, its previous owners, various appraisals, and a definitive description of it. Seymour Freeman, an appraiser of gems in Scottsdale, says his appraisal includes photographs, descriptive details, and, in effect, a record of identity. If the item belonged to one of the famous personages in history or was in a noted collection, it gains value. After all, if J. Paul Getty or Norton Simon owned the piece, that says the piece was highly esteemed by that collector, at least esteemed enough for him to have purchased it. Some of his personal gloss rubs off on the item. Don't get caught in the trap that comes when the dealer says, "Sure, I've a bill of sale and other documents. The owner is out of town right now, though, so I'll forward it to you later." A dealer, if he presents an item for sale, should have all pertinent material and data available then.

No dealer should object to the buyer calling in an independent appraiser or another dealer to inspect the piece. If he says, "No, it's not necessary, why, don't you trust me?" that's a red flag whipping in the wind. No two dealers or appraisers will agree to the dollar about any item's value, but most appraisers say that, depending upon the item's value and the type of item it is, valuations normally will be within 5 or 10 per cent of each other.

The dealer's sales pitch is of importance to the buyer. First, the dealer should know about his merchandise and be able to adequately explain why the item commands the price he is asking. He will talk about its age, condition, distinguishing features, history, and craftsmanship. He'll perhaps cite similar chairs that sold at comparable prices. The collector-buyer should then meticulously research what the dealer told him, checking the huge number of volumes in libraries about similar items, talking with other dealers and collectors, and perhaps calling in an appraiser. The dealer here establishes his credentials with the buyer through his knowledge and, to be sure, nearly all dealers want repeat customers badly.

The dealer should have very nearly as much interest in the satisfaction of his client-customer as in making the one sale. Many times the dealer will tell the collector what reference books to check, which of other dealers in the area are especially knowledgeable in the field, and whatever other resources the collector might call upon to become even more assured that he is making a good purchase.

The reputable dealer is really the only safeguard in these areas because he offers the purchaser recourse. Still, use appraisers often. "It is strange," says San Antonio's Moran, "that the more knowledgeable you become, the more often you turn to other appraisers for their knowledge and insight." Webster's defines *caveat emptor* as, in the New Latin, "let the buyer beware," and in traditional usage, "a principle in commerce: without a warranty the buyer takes the risk of quality upon himself." Let the dealer shoulder that burden.

"If a collector talks to enough other collectors at association meetings and shows, if he talks to dealers and appraisers, he will soon know who the good dealers are," says James Willis of San Francisco. "We all worry about reputations. I wouldn't take a chance on selling anything the least bit shoddy because the buyer will have it in his home. Other collectors will ask him, 'Who sold you that?' He'll say, 'Jim Willis.' This is a very tight business. Somebody sneezes here in San Francisco and they hear it in Paris."

"A reputation for honesty, knowledge, integrity, and fairness means too much to nearly all dealers to tamper with it for one sale," says Thelma Fletcher, an appraiser-dealer in rare books in Salado, Texas. Says another appraiser-dealer, Dick Seelinger of Cuyahoga Falls, Ohio, who specializes in antique and modern firearms, "Reputable dealers have mutual respect for each other. I would rather lose a big deal than jeopardize my reputation. I believe most other dealers feel the same way. Often times, I insist that either before or after a client engages my services that he double-check with the National Rifle Association experts or shop various gun collectors' meetings to compare prevailing prices."

Donald R. Thompson, an El Paso appraiser of Indian art, firearms, and contemporary Western art, adds, "To stay in business the dealer must know the market value of what he sells. He knows his merchandise better than anyone else and his expert advice is included in the cost of the purchase." He says, too, that the dealer's opinion and advice must be checked with other dealers, appraisers, and collectors before the buyer is to consider the dealer fully knowledgeable.

Strangely, it is as difficult to find the good dealer as it is to find the good buy. Herman Herst, Jr., the highly esteemed dean of philately, cautions, "There are far too many who style themselves experts without any justification. There are many mail order firms with no philatelic knowledge whatsoever selling cheap stamps in mail order catalogs, with slick inferences of their investment value when they are next to worthless. To be a stamp dealer, one need pass no test nor have any qualifications or capital . . . . The number of misdescribed, overpriced, and incorrectly identified stamps sold daily to gullible buyers is astounding. The average buyer is himself uninformed and though the knowledge is available in dozens of books easily obtained, he seldom takes the trouble to inform himself. When he gets stung, it is difficult to feel sorry for him."

These kinds of cautions come in all fields of collecting. James H. Cohen, a numismatics appraiser-dealer and a member of the United States Assay Commission, says the buyer must always be wary of dealers. "I feel that many dealers in coins are not truly responsible judges of an item's worth. There are no real restrictions on just what constitutes a knowledgeable dealer. Actually, it is a rather bad situation."

Still, the good and reputable dealer can easily be the collector's greatest asset, so these cautions are to merely help the collector find those dealers he wants. John Klep, an appraiser who owns an art gallery in Houston and who has represented Christie's of London in the Southwest, says that "a dealer can be judged (1) by his credentials, (2) by his experience, and (3) by his reputation in the community and in his profession." He defines the dealer's obligations to the buyer as that primarily of a businessman because, he says, most dealers cannot be regarded as responsible judges of an item's worth and are content to be the businessman, not the merchandising expert.

But once the collector finds a dealer or two who meet the criteria, the dealers can be of inestimable assistance. Some dealers will offer their clients the use of an ultraviolet or black light to help detect restorations and repaintings. Others will guide the collector to the proper reference books, the best collecting organizations and associations, to other reputable dealers and appraisers. The dealer survives and prospers because of repeat business, because of his reputation and loyal clientele.

The experts agree that the reliable dealer should be used as a scout, a seeker of the item you choose to collect. Says appraiser Warren Case, "Most dealers are honest and wise enough to collect customers as well as objects."

A good practice for any collector, after establishing a dealer's credentials, is to openly seek his help. Here, honesty is important. James Willis, who owns an African art gallery in San Francisco, says that he reacts to the manner in which people approach him, in how they treat him. "If a buyer comes in with that chip on his shoulder, with the approach and look that says that he figures I'm trying to screw him, well, the chances are he won't get any breaks from me.

"But if a buyer honestly wants my help in building a collection, wants to become a knowledgeable collector, and if he is willing to work with me, I'll break my back for him. We'll spend time going over areas of collecting, determining what he likes, what it costs. I'll show him as much as I can, I'll loan him books, and well, whatever it is I can do to help him, I will.

"Dealers do have profit margins, of course, so let's say that I just purchased a number of fine pieces. This certain collector has purchased a couple of pieces from me before and I know what he wants. Say he had been in a few days earlier to tell me that he had $700 to spend. So I have a piece that I probably could get $900 for, but because I know this collector will be back again, that he will appreciate a good buy and know that he is getting it, well, I can sell him that piece for $700. I may have to work harder at selling some of the other pieces in that lot to come out as well as I'd like, but I'll do it."

Normally, dealers have the advantage over the collector-buyer in that they seldom need to sell any particular item to any individual. There are exceptions. Book dealer Howell talks of the Bible he bought at an auction in London. "I figured that I had three prospective buyers. But one had experienced a change in his area of interest. Another said he would buy it, but a day later called back to say that he had discovered he already had a copy. The third, well, it's not clear yet whether he will buy it or not." He may, he allows, own that Bible for far longer than he would like.

Howell operates in that rarefied atmosphere of hundreds of thousands of dollars, but even when collectors are spending that kind of money and obviously know something about collecting, the dealer can and should play a huge role. He talks about the experiences of one of his clients, a not-too-experienced collector who bought a highly prized rare book at auction for $220,000. "The young man came in to show me his great buy," says Howell. "But auctions are where dealers feel at home, an area that is part of the dealer's world. I could have saved him a lot of money."

Before World War II, dealers accounted for about 90 per cent of sales, but estimates now put their share close to 50 per cent. The auctions, antique shows, exhibitions, and flea markets all have cut into their share of the market. Yet dealers can perform exceptionally well in any of those areas. "The amateur-Sunday buyer has to compete with the professional if he is to do well," says Henry Cordier, Los Angeles' ranking appraiser-dealer in objets d'art. "The amateur needs all of the help he can get. I don't think collecting can be viewed as an investment by him, though some people do awfully well."

What these dealers are saying is that if the collector puts his trust in them, the collector will not only learn more, and receive full value, but he'll possess a solid protection against the misrepresented work. As philatelist Herst says, "The dealer's obligation is to represent the stamp being sold in its proper condition, to call attention to any faults it may have, and to stand behind the stamp without limit of time and with an offer to refund the full price if competent authorities ever pronounce the stamp to be other than as represented when sold. Few dealers possess this policy. It worked with my firm for over forty years, and as a result, we have been successful from the day we opened the door."

Not all dealers are successful and not all dealers know enough to pledge their firm's standing behind a sale. "A lot of dealers collected themselves into the business," says Moran. "They decided the best way to cash in on their collections was to open a shop. Most of these dealers are great storehouses of misinformation." Use the care in selecting a dealer, he says, that you'd use in choosing a doctor or lawyer.

Just as the dealers of the New York art crowd have little in common with the antique dealer in the California mountains, the practices vary widely from collectible to collectible, though all dealers must finally buy, sell and merchandise. In Sophy Burnham's book, *The Art Crowd,* the dealer hardly stands as the model businessman. She zeros in on New York City and says that savagery in the art market forced some dealers to form the Art Dealers' Association in 1962. She talks of how dealers have shifting price structures for different customers, how prices are hiked through collusion with unsuspecting and unknowing museums, how auctions aid dealers in establishing artificially high values for a painter's work, and how the dealer, anticipating his client's demand for a "good discount" or a "deal," adjusts his prices. "Most of these practices are against the law . . . they occur anyway.

"And this is why the public is advised, if buying High Art, to deal with galleries that belong to the Art Dealers' Association . . . This small group of (then) 85 dealers . . . are committed to some basic honesty about their art. Not that other galleries may not have exquisite items for sale—but one must be careful. And not that an ADA dealer may not overcharge for a picture—but the client is protected from the most nefarious behavior. The ADA, imperfect as it is, remains almost the only protection available to an inexperienced customer . . . . Absence from ADA membership, therefore, means something. The advice is so simple that many people refuse to believe it." Yet, the ADA has not been strongly entrenched across the country. Only one gallery in San Francisco belongs.

Most dealers represent and push certain painters, which makes it advantageous to them to keep the prices of that painter's work moving upward. There are two good devices to assure this. First, if a dealer can convince an upstanding and well-regarded client to donate one of the painter's works to a museum—or, better yet, convince the museum to buy it—that vote of respect from the museum creates standing for the artist in his community. It is not unheard for a dealer, through some ploy, to donate the work himself. After all, if 10 paintings are worth $200 each before the artist's enshrinement in the museum and then suddenly become worth, say, $2,000 each, the $19,000 profit for the dealer and artist make their gift one that is indeed charitable.

Auctions can be used in much the same manner. Again, the purpose is to establish the painter as an artist of worth whose paintings each command thousands of dollars. It works this way: Submit one of the artist's works for auction. For our example, figure the dealer owns the painting. He gets one of his friends or associates to bid on the work, while yet another insider bids him up. The painting is knocked down for $5,000. The dealer mysteriously recovers his painting, loses his 18 per cent commission to the auction house, but has moved well along in establishing a higher value for his artist's works. After all, when the next would-be customer comes in, out comes the auction catalog and . . .

Dealers can promote booming prices, too. The Corey Gallery on San Francisco's Fisherman's Wharf has been pushing a local artist, Cucaro, for years. The gallery touts him as a rival to the late Pablo Picasso; nearly every other authority sees Cucaro as something less. Yet Corey prices Cucaro's work up in the thousands of dollars. Here is the example of the dealer-created phenomenon. Cucaro is not represented as anything but Cucaro; neither, though, will Corey consider buying back his paintings at the price.

Another example is the booming value of the paintings of Jesse Allen, the house painter of Muldoon Elder. Allens have become the darlings of corporate offices, and in 12 years they have zoomed in value from $300 to $350 each on up to the startling levels of $14,000 to $18,000 a painting. Elder will, however, repurchase the Allens. In each instance, the real question is whether these painters will be regarded as among the great painters of this era.

Dealers generally use markups of from 50 to 100 per cent, though that's true mostly where their goods could be considered merchandise—gems, for example. In other collectibles such as antiques, the markup is dependent upon how much the dealer had to pay for the item. In still other collectibles, the dealer sniffs the wind and goes for as much as the market will bear. The collector has to buy as close to the fair price of the item as possible if any short-term profit is to be realized. The markups on diamonds are about 100 per cent so the collector would either have to find a source to buy for him at or near wholesale prices or wait a few years until his gem doubled in value to consider himself at the breakeven point. And, too, dealers who offer "grab bags" of diamonds, coins, or stamps have not been found to offer any bargains. The sizes of their promotional budgets for advertising do not necessarily build integrity or value.

The collector always must be concerned with the quality of his purchase, and, of course, the collector must consider the possibility of fakes, forgeries, and other flim flams. Remember that provenances—the documentation—are more easily produced by the schemers than the work of art itself. Signatures are studied as religiously by the forger as the collector and they are quickly applied to furniture, crystal, and other objets d'art.

Appraising Appraisers

Not many collectors consult appraisers before making buys, not even on major acquisitions. Yet the appraiser holds a unique position in this whole field of valuation and collecting; and he enjoys an intimate involvement with the arts. He stands alone as the only professional who is independent of the whims and desires of the buyer and the seller, and he offers a service that helps the collector get past the worst of the dangers of *caveat emptor.* Most appraisers, because of their stature in their field of expertise, double as dealers, investment advisers, lecturers, authors, or auctioneers.

There are two major associations of personal property appraisers: the American Society of Appraisers (ASA), headquartered in Washington, D.C., and the Appraisers Association of America (AAA), headquartered in New York, N.Y. The ASA tests and certifies its members; those who pass the exams and requirements receive the Senior designation "ASA". The Society is non-profit, international in scope (members in U.S., Canada, England, Australia, Philippines, Puerto Rico, Mexico, etc.) and bases its work on education and research. The AAA, centering its activities in New York City, designates its members with "AAA". Both Societies require adherence to a Code of Ethics. The ASA is especially noted for its present work in establishing (for the first time in the history of the U.S.) an academically-accredited nationwide Valuation Sciences Degree program for all appraisers (whether personal property or real estate). Also, ASA is noted for its unique "stand" (a Resolution adopted in 1971 by its Board of Governors) recommending some form of state regulation (licensing, certification or registration) of all appraisers in order to help protect the public from incompetent or unethical practices.

Appraising is a fast-growing profession that every serious collector should view as a possible career. Today, the ASA has certified less than 200 personal property appraisers, and that includes those in every specialty from objets d'art, paintings, sculpture and classic automobiles to coins, stamps and antiques. Though the ASA has thousands of members, the rest are associated in such areas as the appraisal of real estate, machinery and equipment, and intangibles, such as patents, copyrights, franchises and the like.

To best define the field, ASA has a pretty long Code of Ethics (8 sections, which touch on objectives, appraisers duties and responsibilities, obligations to client and the public, methods, specific unethical practices, and appraisal report preparation). Here's a sample of one statement, about the "Professional Character of Appraisal Practice":

> "The members of the Society are engaged in a professional activity. A profession is based on an organized body of specific knowledge—knowledge not possessed by laymen. It is of such a character that it requires a high degree of intelligence and a considerable expenditure of time and effort to acquire it and to become adept in its application. An appraiser's client, because he does not have the necessary specialized knowledge himself, puts his trust in the appraiser and relies on him to use his professional knowledge and abilities to whatever extent may be necessary to accomplish the objectives of the work. There is no *caveat emptor* principle involved in the relationship between a professional appraiser and his client. Members of the Society recognize this fiduciary relationship."

Today, the best way for a collector to identify one of the leading appraisers is to look for senior members of the ASA. They're listed in the yellow pages, and the best of them are well known to most longtime collectors and dealers. The senior member has established credentials. Not only must he have been in the field as an appraiser—perhaps as a member of the ASA—for five years, he must submit examples of his appraisals and undergo a rigorous day-long examination by a board of senior members. Finally, a person who is a senior member subscribes to the association's code and considers appraising as a profession.

Strangely, many beginning collectors or non-collectors still possess the mistaken belief that appraisers do not warrant fair and reasonable fees, regardless of his level of expertise and the effort he expended in accumulating the knowledge. After all, real estate appraisers often work for brokers and many appraisals are hardly independent decisions. The broker, not the potential home buyer, usually absorbs the appraiser's fee. And in many fields value is not difficult to ascertain; stocks are quoted daily in the newspapers, for example. "People have not yet, at least in our society, accepted the notion that an appraiser's function is as important to them as, say, that of a lawyer or an accountant," says Dexter MacBride, the ASA's executive vice president.

For example, if a collector purchases an antique table for several hundred dollars, paying a premium because of the craftsman who made it, he can hardly afford to subsequently learn that the table is not the genuine article as represented. Too often he will not be able to recoup any money, especially if the dealer knew he was improperly representing the table. The dealer surely will have covered his tracks well enough to elude prosecution. So when a collector starts buying valuable items, the stakes can get terribly high in a hurry. Paintings go for tens of thousands of dollars; so do exquisite examples of French antique furniture. "It's pure foolishness to put your financial future in the hands of a man, an unknown dealer, who stands to profit immensely from your purchase," says rare book expert, Thelma Fletcher.

An example. John Tucker, a Houston appraiser of paintings, was talking about appraising when he was interrupted by a woman who wanted an appraisal on a picture. Tucker was going to tell her that she needed an appointment, but his task was not that time consuming. He was back in a few minutes, "She just paid $400 for a really fine photographic reproduction that had been neatly clipped from a book and then beautifully framed," he grimaced.

Seymour Freeman, the Scottsdale gemologist, says that diamonds can be improved through some intricate doctoring so that no small-town jeweler can possibly detect the work. The touch of a laser beam can do wonders for a flawed diamond. The appraiser of gems truly needs to have gone through the Gemological Institute to be competent. "I go every so often," says Freeman, "just to make sure my ability to compare and contrast stones is as accurate as necessary." Synthetic gems are appearing more frequently, and today some of them take a fine level of knowledge to differentiate between the real thing and the synthetic copy. One man-made ruby can only be detected by a test that destroys the synthetic version.

Appraising is a much more precise business than the layman figures, and appraisers rebel at the idea there's a great deal of guesswork involved. Most agree that there's likely to be a 5 to 10 per cent variance between the valuations of different appraisers. Yet, there's no uniform rate nor any uniform way in which they decide upon the rate for their services. There also is no uniformity in how they present appraisals, though the ASA's senior-member examination and proposed legislation presented to state legislatures would both work to alleviate this situation.

Donald R. Thompson, a senior member of the ASA who specializes in firearms, Indian artworks, and contemporary western art, says, "To buy an item of major importance from an unknown source or questionable individual, a buyer had best employ a rated appraiser who will charge for his services on an hourly or fixed-fee basis, not on a basis which is in any way tied in with the price of the item being purchased. (The fee should reflect) an amount commensurate with the time required to appraise an item and the quality of the appraisal presentation. The appraiser is bound by his code of ethics to give a true monetary evaluation on the subject item and never to base his fee on the amount of his appraisal but on the time and expense outlaid." There's a huge disagreement here among appraisers. Those who belong to ASA are required to adhere to a Code of Ethics which spells out prohibitions against contingency fees, commissions, rebates, division of brokerage commissions, finders or referral fees. Appraisers who do not belong to a society requiring such conduct hold different views.

Thompson adds, "There are two ways an appraiser can err in his estimate of value. He can be too high or too low. In my appraisal, comparables are quoted to bracket an item and the item is evaluated upon its comparable age, condition, size or other criteria, all of which is part of the presentation, and is submitted to the client. The sources of information are detailed. The process of evaluation is clear and complete. Retail and wholesale prices are shown with normal dealer margins quoted.

"There is no reason the presentation could not be submitted as incontrovertible evidence in any court to substantiate the correctness of values given. I do not subscribe to a policy of stating, 'The value of your — is so and so many dollars. Period.' This opens the appraisal to challenge and expensive court costs. Where comparables are shown, processes of conclusions plainly stated, there is no question of individual integrity involved. It is simply, 'Here are my comparables, here are my reasons for the evaluation. Disprove, if you can!' "

Another senior ASA member, philatelist Herst, explains that fees vary, depending on the use for which the appraisal is made and the time and expense involved in making it. "I have charged as little as $25 an hour for a quick appraisal done in my office to $200 per day plus expenses when it involves distant travel."

Other appraisers say they charge from one or two

per cent up to 10 or 25 per cent of the item's value. Nearly all have a $25 to $50 minimum. James H. Cohen of New Orleans says he charges "between $50 and $100 per hour for highly concentrated technical advice." Too, the appraiser's fee is negotiable. Henry Cordier, the respected fine arts appraiser in Los Angeles, says, his fee "depends on the value of the object. Let's say a very minimum of $50, but a few hundred dollars would be all right if the appraiser has to do research and the object warrants it."

But for the fee the collector not only gains the most informed judgment of the value of his item and dispels his worries over being taken by the seller, he also gets a full description. "We do guarantee to defend our appraisals in court," say Ralph and Terry Kovel, authors and appraisers of American antiques. Still, the collector must be aware that different appraisers have different sets of standards.

Some appraisers might establish the value and then offer to purchase the item, which leads to a situation that could present a conflict of interest. This is the reason most appraisers contend appraisers should work for hourly fees and not for fees based on an item's value. One appraiser says that situations can occur to create difficulties for appraisers and that they crop up quite unexpectedly. "I ran into what appeared to be the bonnet off the top of a grandfather clock that had been converted into a small chest with 13 small drawers," she says. "I told the woman what I thought it was and that I'd pay her $75 for it, since she wanted to sell it. That was also the appraisal fee I was charging her for valuing of her items.

"I always believe that an appraiser has to travel often to determine what the market is doing elsewhere in the country. So the next time I was back East I was doing the museums. I had already checked all of my books and talked with all of my friends but I had not been able to come up with precisely what this small chest was. But then I saw an identical copy tucked back away in this museum. I got the docent and she said it was a Chippendale chest. We found a date and suddenly I knew I had an item that was worth about $1,500. When I returned home I called the woman from whom I had bought the item and asked her if she wanted it back or whether I could pay her a fair price for it. She, of course, was delighted with the money."

Appraisers do not find too many items that stump them, though they all routinely call other appraisers in when items go beyond their area of expertise. Today it is still a very tight, small fraternity, and it's questionable whether enough people are calling in appraisers consistently enough for the field to experience dramatic growth. If state laws are passed that will give the appraiser an established position, then it's quite possible it will become a profession where there is great demand for services.

"Appraisers are much like doctors back in the 1790 to 1810 era," says Houston's Tucker. "They were still pulling teeth then. But at least we're moving up in stature although we're still quasi-professional. To me a profession is not a money making thing, though we all recognize a certain amount of money is necessary to live properly. Appraising is a way of life. It's ridiculous that a person such as a public accountant is certified because he must work with your money and charge fees in the hundreds of dollars. But you take a man like me—or anyone who hangs up an appraiser's shingle—and he passes on million-dollar paintings."

Appraising is one of the acceptable methods of dealing with fine works of art daily, though the person might not have the money to purchase them. The discipline offers all of the aesthetic satisfactions of museum curating, collecting, teaching, and writing. Appraisers earn reputations as surely as dealers and collectors. Dealers seek the best of them out, as do insurance companies and trust account managers. A first-rate appraiser's opinion or judgment is valued in courts.

Not often do appraisers find themselves on the spot with their opinions fully challenged and hugely in doubt. Normally intensive research and study can untie the riddle. There are, however, the great historical puzzles.

The case of the Twentieth-Century Vermeers, as chronicled by Frank Arnau in *The Art of the Faker,* raises more questions than were answered by the confession of Hans van Meegeren. The Dutch painter-dealer had worked for years to perfect his "Vermeer style," and for years van Meegeren's works stood as Vermeers, until he produced *The Disciples of Emmanus.* It purportedly was a work by Vermeer in his obscure youth, which had been unexpectedly uncovered. Dr. Abraham Bredus, an 80-year-old art historian and authority on Dutch masters, subjected the paintings to the four tests of authenticity as deemed necessary then: (1) Resistance of the paints to alcohol and other solvents, (2) Evidence of white lead in the white portions, (3) X-ray examination of the substratum, and (4) Microscopic and spectroscopic examination of the principal pigments. Though van Meegeren said he painted several Vermeer imitations, confessed and was convicted, there still remains doubt as to whether all of the paintings van Meegeren claims to have been his work truly were. Writes Arnau, "Thirteen years after the Amsterdam court's decision (1947), the van Meegeren case is still shrouded in the same cloak of obscurity which characterized the life of the man himself."

Significantly, art historians and experts differed roundly on whether the paintings were original Vermeers or whether an imposter was making his name through the contention that he had created works of such stupendous genius. Regardless, the historians who surveyed and studied the works were unable to definitively determine the authenticity of the paintings. To a lesser degree, that same problem confronts appraisers today.

John Mayhill, assistant publisher of the *Tri-State Trader,* a hobby and antiques newspaper begun in 1968 that now has a circulation of about 30,000 readers, explains, "One of the real dangers in the antique collecting field is reproductions being sold as authentic pieces. We try to screen our advertisers as much as is humanly possible, but occasionally we get one who tries to sell a reproduction as an antique. It's a big rip-off. We demand reproductions be marked as such and if we find someone passing one off as authentic, he goes on our blacklist.

"There are many manufacturers, such as Coca-Cola, American Heritage, etc., who clearly mark their reproductions but there are others who have taken antique molds, manufactured reproductions and then sold them as antiques. We have joined other antique publications and antique dealers everywhere to fight this fraudulent activity. It has to be stopped or it could ruin the business."

Today many dealers double as appraisers, which is an acceptable practice only if the dealer has no fiduciary interest in the transaction and has sufficient standing and knowledge for his opinion to stand if challenged. In fact, if a progression were to be drawn of how careers flourish, it would probably go collector, dealer, appraiser, and then author, lecturer, and historian.

One of the best insights into the world of collecting comes from an understanding of the kinds of people who are intimately involved with it. There is no one route to expertise, and the appraisers and dealers have varied backgrounds. Most of them view their careers as extensions of their private lives. It's significant that formal education is not a prerequisite to becoming one of the most highly esteemed authorities. For example, there's Mervyn Cohn, who was a pawnbroker for 27 years; the past five years he has been a dealer-appraiser in gems. Cohn's expertise is based on his years of experience and the Gemological Institute of America's home-study course. Or consider the courtly, erudite Henry K. Cordier, who represents the fifth generation of his family to deal in the antique and art field. He's one of the West Coast's most respected appraisers of fine arts and other personal property. Though both men double as retail dealers, they possess a common belief in the rigid adherence to the highest standards of their profession.

Ruth Murphy, a Lansing, Michigan, appraiser of antiques, has worked in the field for the past 17 years. She was a dealer for 10 years, a parttime appraiser for three years, and for the past six years it has been her fulltime pursuit. She says her original involvement in the field was "recreational therapy. I needed to take my mind off the problems of raising a Hemophiliac son," she says. Her fascination with antiques and with the people involved in the field grew, which pushed her into "the great responsibility" or professionally helping others.

For others, they were exposed to the field early in life. Ruth Burns of Shawnee Mission, Kansas, says, "My interest began as a child, but really developed after graduation from college and the inheritance of many antiques. It developed as a hobby, then became all consuming, and upon widowhood, a business as an appraiser." She has lectured on Wedgwood since 1961, and for the past eight years has taught classes on how to identify and value antiques.

Her explanation of why she has become so immersed in the field reveals much about how consuming appraising can become. "I like people and get along with them," she says. "I've studied on my own and in museums in this country and in Europe as one in organized groups. I am a member of the International Wedgwood Seminar, the Wedgwood Society of London, the Buten Museum of Wedgwood, the Heye Foundation, the Cowboy Hall of Fame, the Museum of Northern Arizona and others. They all publish materials to add to my store of knowledge. I get 15 publications per month pertaining to the fields of art and antiques, and I read them carefully. I have a personal library in those fields, which exceeds 2,000 books for reference, all of which I have read and studied. I know where to find the answers to most things that I do not know. I am the appraiser for the Kansas City Museum on donations for tax purposes."

She considers herself expert in the appraising and identification of "antiques and collectibles and their value in today's market, particularly English pottery and porcelain, i.e. Wedgwood, Worcester glass, European, American, and American Indian arts and crafts."

Nate Bradlin of Beachwood, Ohio, exemplifies what one expects in an appraiser. He defines his area of expertise as "the making, repairing, varnishing, rebuilding, appraising, and buying and selling of violins, violas, and cellos." The 56-year-old craftsman came to his profession through his love of good music. "From early childhood through high school I played the violin and later the viola. At the age of 13, I met a local violin craftsman who did some repair work on one of my damaged violas. We became friends and from that I became intrigued and interested."

At 13, Bradlin entered his apprenticeship with the renowned Carl Ackley of Youngstown, Ohio. For three and one-half years Bradlin's expertise with and love for the instruments grew. "Through the ensuing years while I was in college and then the Army, I visited several known violin makers, and read many, many books. During my tenure with Ackley we saw and repaired, bought and sold many instruments. Most of the professional orchestra people patronized us. Since 1946 I have been doing the same work from my home here near Cleveland."

In the past 10 years Bradlin has visited Europe several times to study with some other master craftsmen. "In the years, 1967, 1969, 1970, and 1972, I studied with today's oldest living violin maker, Professor Guiseppe Moduado of Santa Agata, Catania, Sicily." He also talked to and studied with Mario Colucci of Cremona, Guiseppe Lucci in Rome, and others in Vienna, Switzerland, and Germany. He made several visits to London where he frequented Sotheby's, Christies, and Hills.

Bradlin's greatest loves are for his own hand-made violins. One, which he produced from 140-year-old wood he found in Italy, is "an exact copy of one of the Guarnerius of 1734, and which the late Fernando Sacconi claimed to have one of the finest tones he ever heard in a contemporary instrument."

Other appraisers possess a blend of the craftsman's art and the competence that comes through long years of study. Lyle Downey, who for nearly 30 years was a professor at the University of California's San Jose campus, also still works in a large and well-appointed shop where he rebuilds and restores antique furniture and other works of art. He defines his area of expertise as the "field of music, especially stringed instruments; art in general, but in particular painted and sculptured art and carved stone items; furniture and house furnishings." It at first sounds like a terribly wide area of expertise, but Downey's background is truly varied and interesting.

"I lived and grew up in immediate proximity—across one lot—to a stone construction shop and had training conducted by my father and grandfather. At eight years of age I was apprenticed to a cabinet maker and continued work with wood and mechanics through a technical junior and senior high school and two years of university." And, too, from the age of four he was consistently studying and playing music.

He received his A.B. degree from James Millikin University and completed three years of civil engineering at the University of Illinois, Urbana. Then, he earned his bachelor's and master's degrees in music from the American Conservatory, Chicago. He was a professional cellist with the Chicago Civic Symphony, the Katz and Balaban Theaters in Chicago, Peoria, Joliet and Decatur, Illinois. In the 1930s he began his studies for a doctorate in music at the Eastman School of Music, Rochester, New York, and finally earned it in 1942 at the University of Iowa, Iowa City. In 1954 and 1955 he was involved in research study in administration at Stanford University.

Yet Downey claims to "operate mostly in the 'peanut league'." He says it is "presently a crazy business." His expanding interests have followed his "inquisitive instinct, desire, and need to learn about things that intrigue me. I look for opportunities to explain certain things, items, usages, values, and the discovery, invention, and development'' (of other items).

It does not, however, take this kind of formal background or highly developed craftsman's eye to make a fine appraiser or dealer. Some of the most highly respected experts have literally learned their trade by self-study, or by working with experts, such as their husbands. Catherine Bullowa of Philadelphia and Thelma Fletcher of Salado, Texas, are grand examples.

Thelma picked up her husband's rare book dealership when he died and has established her own reputation. She's a wonderfully warm and engaging woman who, when most women her age think of retirement, possesses an infectious energy and enthusiasm to match her expertise. She often flies to either coast to consult with other experts or to work on appraisals. ''It's a grand life,'' she beams.

Catherine Bullowa found herself in much the same position when her husband died in 1953. ''I was in medical research and teaching, and I was used to handling microscopes and trained in dealing with detailed information. My late husband was one of the foremost numismatists in the world, and his teachings were detailed and specific,'' she says. ''I have been considered a knowledgeable numismatist in my own right, having been in this business since 1952, but after my husband's death I continued to get helpful knowledge from experts in fields in which I felt insecure.''

She, like so many authorities, knows enough to ask for help when it's needed and enjoys giving assistance herself. ''I pride myself in being able to help people make decisions along my specialized lines as well as kindred ones. At times there may be an appraisal needed for estates left to parties who are not knowledgeable, and here the appraiser is most necessary, to make sure the person or parties get the proper values for the entire collection in writing.''

There does not appear to be any single common denominator that distinguishes the established dealer or appraiser, unless it's a willingness to learn about items and subjects that fascinate them greatly. Here, again, is the dictum that most authorities emphasize: select your field of collecting with great care. A great many of today's respected dealers and appraisers gravitated naturally into their careers following years of collecting, of handling items, studying, browsing, talking, listening. "You don't see many items you haven't read about or inspected before," says Ms. Fletcher.

As appraising moves ever closer to becoming an established profession with state-mandated regulations, the consumers' confidence in procuring competent appraisers should increase. But there are still areas of the profession's practices and procedures where appraisers hold conflicting opinions. They figure their fees in different ways; an hourly rate with expenses, a percentage of the value of the item appraised, or some combination of the two. And too, whether appraisers should lead double lives, that of the independent assessor of value along with, say, either investment adviser or dealer.

First, consider the question of whether the appraiser might also act as an investment adviser. Says Herman Herst, the dean of philatelic appraisers, "It is often done in the philatelic field, but I decline such ventures. Our hobby is literally strewn with investment counselors who give bad advice, by design or by accident, and I want no part of it." Agrees Hawaiian Tim Morrow, "I do not think that is within his realm, nor do I think it is ethical to do so." Or, as Margaret Hilmes of Overland Park, Kansas, puts it, "In the strictest sense, an appraiser should be independent of any involvement other than appraisal."

The dispute has appraisers equally split on the question. Many appraisers simply say, "of course," to the question, "Can an appraiser be asked to serve a wider function; i.e., that of an investment adviser or counselor, a tipster to good deals?" Lowell Collins of Houston says, "Yes—most definitely." Adds John Klep, also of Houston, "Certainly, if asked to do so. I would encourage this habit which, unfortunately, few collectors have adopted."

There are many who feel that the appraiser might become the adviser, with certain qualifications. Winslow Ames says, "Adviser or counselor, yes, if at an agreed upon fee. Tipster, no. That is the job of a chum or old crony, and it isn't professional." Robert Kaller of Carmel, California, says, "(The appraiser) may well take on other functions, but not as an appraiser. In short, he would be donning another hat." James H. Cohen of New Orleans counsels, "Yes, an appraiser could serve as an investment adviser, et cetera, provided there is no conflict of interest."

Always there is concern of conflicts of interest. Donald Thompson of El Paso argues, "An appraiser's opinion on investment value should be of great value to his client and his counsel should be fundamentally sound. If asked as to sources of good values on items covered by his particular discipline, I see no ethical reason to withhold such information. If your words 'tipster to good deals' means acting as a tout, presumably for a commission, then acting as a tipster would, in my opinion, be unethical in the extreme. If on the other hand an appraiser is asked by a client to help in finding a buyer for an item or items he has appraised, this would be entirely in order." The line is, after all, a terribly fine one to draw.

The dispute over whether the appraiser's fee is to be based strictly on time or on the value of the item is not quite so distinctly drawn. The ASA takes the position that fees are to be based on previously agreed upon charges for time and expenses. There is also a secondary question here as to whether dealers can act as appraisers and how their fees fit into the picture.

Thompson says, "The fee should be an amount commensurate with the time required to appraise an item and the quality of the appraisal presentation. The appraiser is bound by his code of ethics to give a true monetary evaluation of the subject item and never to base his fee on the amount of his appraisal, but on the time and expense outlaid. While a dealer would or should have enough basic knowledge to form an accurate appraisal, the question of personal gain is injected into the opinion. This is just what a rated appraiser is barred from by his ethics, so it follows that dealers would have no ethical consideration to eliminate the matter of personal gain from influencing their opinions."

J. Lee Drexler, a 31-year-old appraiser in the New York City area, says, "I feel there's a conflict of interest if anyone tries to appraise and then buy something. Even a saint would be tempted to give a low appraisal. I only appraise. My company does no buying or selling. The appraiser's obligation is to his client, but he must be totally honest. I've had clients try to have me raise or lower my prices to suit their interests. My stock answer is, I'll give you as high (or as low) an appraisal as I feel will be accepted by the Internal Revenue Service and which, of course, is honest. I never let my clients influence me to do anything that is not proper. I recently turned down a high fee to appraise a set of tapes because I felt they had virtually no value. Three weeks later I discovered that the I.R.S. had a new regulation which stated that for a donation of tapes, their value was equal only to the cost of the tape itself ($6) with no extra value. I was very glad I had refused this job. Appraising prices, however, can vary a great deal depending on the need of the appraisal. A selling price is always lower than a retail purchase price. My fee is $50 an hour with a $75 minimum charge. I also charge an additional rate for researched fine art and jewelry."

Another New York City appraiser, Stefan Cavallo, whose area of expertise includes the contents of homes or estates, including fine art, and recently the content appraisal of three large hotels in Washington, D.C., and New York City, figures his fee differently. It varies "from ½ to 1½% of F.M.V. (full market value) of the contents, according to the number of items and difficulty of identification." Lee Schreiber of Rosemont, Pa., an appraiser of antiques and objects of art, considers that "a truly competent appraiser should receive a fee between 5 and 10 per cent."

Yet in terms of the fee charged, most appraisers feel that it can and should be negotiated before the work is done. And even then most of them agree that the negotiations should be based on time spent and actual expenses incurred. Most appraisers have minimum fees that start at $20 and go as high as $250, and most charge from $20 to $50 an hour, or say, $25 for a "quick verbal appraisal," as one puts it.

It is wise to remember that there are several reasons for calling in an appraiser. First, there is the question of authenticating and valuing a perspective purchase. Second, appraising has much to do with tax situations that arise with donations of items or even capital gains upon the sale of the item. Too, there is the ever-present need to have the contents of a home appraised for insurance purposes. This is of much greater importance than most people realize, especially considering the ever increasing crime rate. Most insurance companies have riders they attach for fine arts, antiques and jewelry. The cost varies greatly according to the section of country or city involved, but the savings can be immense, if a burglary or loss occurs, for whatever reason. Without the appraised value of antiques listed with the insurance company, the already valuable pieces that are appreciating in value will still be depreciated by insurance companies, just as newly bought furniture is.

Counselors on Collectibles

Any collector continually seeks advice, whether from other collectors, well-informed or misinformed dealers, knowledgeable appraisers, or even the trusting spouse who must be kept trusting. As always, some of the advice will be excellent, some horrendous. And because there's so much of it floating around so cheaply, few collectors consider paying for it. In any number of particular circumstances, however, he should.

There is no local office similar to that of a stock market brokerage firm with banks of desks of brokers, who daily digest information from the firm's analysts and all other sources they can develop. These brokers are salesmen who command a fee for buying or selling in the market, and because they deal in the market daily many people come up believing most of them are investment advisers. Nothing could be farther from the truth. The point, of course, is that advice must be sound to be of value, and because a person holds a certain job means little about his level of knowledge.

For example, nearly ten years ago I decided to write an article for the *National Observer,* on the difficulties of becoming a licensed stock broker. I had only dabbled in the market and my grounding in economics was hardly sound. Yet in New York I took a two-day cram course—with no preparation—and the following day took the licensing examination that would qualify me to buy and sell stocks right along-side the Loebs, Lehmans, and Goodbodys. I passed with flying colors and wrote, to my mind, a revealing article about just how little stock brokers had to know about the value of stocks. And they have to know almost nothing; they do have to know how to stay clear of government red tape.

As Ruth Murphy, Michigan's only appraiser in

personal property in the ASA, says, "Most people—dealers, appraisers, collectors—claim much more expertise than they possess." There are no qualifications necessary to become a dealer or an appraiser in most states—only the money for the shingle.

This chapter deals with investment advisers and the services they offer collectors. Despite the cautions and explanations as to why any collector should view advice with a jaundiced eye, there are many dealers and appraisers highly qualified to serve as investment advisers. Many of them routinely serve clients as an integral part of their business, others refuse to, and some may only in particular instances. Still others feel very strongly that a person should not become a serious collector until he has the personal knowledge and confidence to risk his own money. To them, the profit in collecting is secondary to the joy the person receives from buying and owning works of art.

Let's discuss the circumstances that might warrant the collector seeking professional advice.

First, the collector finds himself greatly taken with, for example, the fragile beauty of antique Wedgwood, and the collector also believes that now is a good time to purchase several pieces. Still, he possesses neither the time nor the inclination to become truly knowledgeable himself.

Though the collector has studied his field for years, he finds himself making a major purchase—at least a major purchase according to his purse. An adviser could be of great value in reinforcing his judgment, or in helping the collector better understand the vagaries of the marketplace.

Second, the collector has decided to make substantial purchases of the work of a particular artist. Most buys will be made at auction, and he wishes to have the dispassionate mind and skill of a professional to help make his purchases at the proper price and to temper his enthusiasm and passion.

Third, the collector wants to build a collection of, for example, gems where he must beat the 50 to 100 per cent markup to the dealer's retail price to possess a reasonable chance to turn a profit within a reasonable period of time. He needs an adviser who has access to the wholesale price of items, and the expertise to make wise purchases.

Fourth, for years the collector has studied and browsed, always moving along the periphery of the field. His success in building a collection of value has been indifferent. But he has come to know well one dealer or appraiser in whom he strongly believes. Many people are successful in life if only because they have the ability to properly choose in which people to place their trust—and money.

There may be other areas in which the collector may choose to select a financial adviser, but it is important to recognize that many of the authorities in many of the collectible fields are strongly opposed to such a liaison. These experts contend that the purpose of collecting has more to do with the sheer enjoyment and fealty to art than a preoccupation with dollars.

This chapter will include a discussion on how much some investment advisers charge clients, what the client should expect for the fee, how to select an adviser, and how to allay worries about an adviser's competence and expertise. This method of collecting does not offer the rewards nor knowledge as does the process when the collector pursues first knowledge and then items for his collection. However, it does offer the person who has enough money to make his use of a counselor advisable the chance to have his money working for him while he learns under the tutelage of an expert.

Yet some of the most highly respected authorities believe a collector should never, never use an adviser in such a manner. Says Warren E. Cox, the 80-year-old president of Warren E. Cox Associates in New York and the author of a book on pottery and porcelain that has sold more than 100,000 copies, "If you keep your eye on the dollar, you cannot see the art." He's a perfect example of this school of thought that he, not coincidentally, expresses so well. He flatly states, "Don't call in an appraiser (or adviser). Don't buy until you know yourself. An appraiser can be used as an adviser just as a 'marriage broker' can be called in about love."

He counsels the prospective buyer who is looking for a bargain or deals to try to buy his items near the wholesale price level, "There are no price structures in either art appreciation—or love. Good deals have little to do with real taste or art appreciation."

Officially Cox rates himself an appraiser of Near and Far Eastern art, but over his lengthy career his expertise has expanded to many allied fields. Like so many authorities, he minces few words, "Value depends on three things. One, quality and taste. Two, what you know. And three, what the buyer or seller (whichever you aren't) knows." He gets frustrated with today's preoccupation with turning a profit. "Damn the investing angle. It will take care of itself if you work. The returns are excellent." Here again, his career proves that; he is, by any measure, a very wealthy man.

John Tucker, a wry, salty Texan whose knowledge of paintings has won him the respect of other appraisers and dealers, shares many of Cox's views. There are not that many appraisers who do nothing but appraisals, but Tucker's view is that of many professionals in other disciplines. "My work constitutes a profession, and there's little difference to me as to whether I personally own the great works of art so long as I can live and work with them. Sure, there have been fortunes made and there are fortunes to be made, but the collector must be knowledgeable. A work of art is conceived in pleasure or emotion and it should be viewed in pleasure. There's no other earthly reason for possessing a work of art. For example, a picture needs talking about and that talking must be intelligent. The artist comes into it. The ideal is to know the artist intimately, but if the collector cannot know the artist he at least must know his work intimately. That never happens when an adviser is used."

Then with his sure touch of wit and humor, Tucker explains how he and not many wealthy collectors will be remembered by history. "I'm going to be a part of art history because I use 500-year paper. Strange, but some of the richest men I know use poor paper. I only use 100 per cent rag bond. A note may cost me 35 cents, but it's one of my foibles. Still, I know my records will persist." He points out that many people really don't want to properly use an appraiser or adviser. "When you tell a buyer that he got bilked or made a poor purchase, most become outraged and tell me to my face—or someone else later—that I'm full of bunk."

Men like Cox and Tucker could be considered the purists, men whom would have all people innately possess what is truly a rare quality. For after all, the learned and practiced "wise eye" that distinguishes quality and value flawlessly is something that not all people can gain. Although some violinists may practice devotedly, there are only so many virtuosos and only so many who play first chair. There are only so many skilled linguists, Pulitzer Prize-winning writers, and old masters in the art world. For everyone who made it, there must be thousands who try equally hard, but somehow fame, success, and riches escape them. It is for these people, who must constitute a large number of prospective successful collectors, that investment advisers will be of service.

The extent to which a collector might wish to employ an adviser turns largely upon the items he has chosen to collect, and of course, the amount of money he wishes to spend. Seymour Freeman, a gemologist who operates as an appraiser-dealer-adviser from his store in Scottsdale, Arizona, explains that if a person chooses to invest in rare gems such as diamonds, jade, rubies, opals, and sapphires, he has little choice but to choose an agent to buy for him and to advise him on his purchases.

"It's definitely worth the money to get an expert in this field," he says, adding that most times the small-town jeweler or very nearly any salesman has an inadequate store of knowledge and expertise. "There are diamonds that have been improved by lasers, where most times the doctoring will escape the jeweler's loop. The same is true for jade when the color has been enhanced. This kind of examination requires such instruments as high-powered microscopes and spectroscopes."

More commonly the problems arise because a jeweler improperly grades a diamond. Freeman says he returns to the gemological institute for a refresher course every few years. "It's possible to lose sight of standards, which can be subjective to a degree," he explains.

Diamonds, of course, have been and continue to be exceptionally fine investments. Regardless of where the wealthy and *nouveau riche* exist in the world—it was Japan in the early 1970s and now it is the Middle East—the allure of the perfect diamond creates continuing demand. Prices last year moved up about 35 per cent and that was not an unusually good performance.

"But if a man buys five diamonds for $1200 from a retail jeweler who charges him the full markup—his cost of doing business and his profit margin—then the purchaser would have to wait several years to break even." Most diamonds of a full carat or more cost thousands of dollars and Freeman agrees that it is unlikely that the dealer-adviser could do much for the person without, say, $10,000 or $50,000, which he could invest and hold for a few years.

"The fees the adviser charges are negotiable," he says. "I would guess that 10 per cent would not be an unusual figure. It would be more than fair to the purchaser who then is buying at the wholesale market and would more than likely reach a break even point within a year. The fee might go as low as 2 to 5 per cent, depending upon how difficult it was for the adviser-dealer to find what he is looking for. The fee might also depend upon the relationship, its duration, and the amount of freedom the dealer is given."

Freeman says that he knows one layman who did gain access to the wholesale market for investment purposes. "He got his brains knocked out because he made a couple of bad buys," he says. The percentage the adviser tacks on is the price of doing business because gemology has become a scientific art. It has developed in only the past 50 years; before then an expert could not say with any degree of certainty that a ruby was a ruby, at least not with the certainty required in court. "In this field the investment adviser is a necessity, and if he is a good one, then the investor has an excellent opportunity to see fine returns," adds Freeman.

Nate Bradlin, the Ohioan who is a dealer, appraiser, and adviser on stringed instruments, says "the quick answer" to how a person might become a serious investor without spending years to accumulate knowledge is that "he should avail himself of an expert in the field who would charge him on a preset agreement and act as his teacher, confidant, and guiding counselor, much like a good bond broker-counselor."

In Bradlin's field, like Freeman's, experience has no substitute. "There is no man alive who could pinpoint every violin shown to him," he says. "One must know the very difficult patterns of the many schools of the past. One must have worked on instruments. One must have seen authentic specimens." He says most dealers cannot be regarded as responsible judges of an instrument's worth. "Only a crafted maker who has studied the art, who has followed closely the international and national market sales of good instruments, and who is daily involved can make a judgment. Many fine music dealers are some of my best customers."

He explains that his role differs with different customers. "As a reputable dealer and appraiser, I find that to be competitive I must give some people—professionals, teachers, and orchestra members who regularly patronize my business—a slight discount off list. Others, such as large purchasers like schools and colleges, 20 per cent off list is about standard in the trade." Those discounts are not standard for the investing collector as he seldom buys merchandise but rather fine instruments. "In the case of the serious collector we get a fee ranging from 5 to 20 per cent, depending upon a preset arrangement."

The craftsman adds that in many instances the purchaser-collector should seek out a second appraisal, particularly if the instrument is expensive and its lineage is at all in doubt. "No reputable appraiser questions a buyer's wanting a double-check . . . because any good violin by a good maker and authenticated with papers is today and will be more so in the future a good investment. Therefore, speculating on these type purchases is like putting money in the bank at the highest interest for your best return, which really is not speculating in that sense of the word."

Yet, there are few truly qualified investment counselors in collectibles. Henry K. Cordier, the Los Angeles fine arts appraiser, says few appraisers act as art consultants. In an address he gave before the ASA's international conference in 1975, he said, "If there is such a person as a professional art investment counselor at all, he certainly practices a rare profession. I am not talking about the art dealer who kindles the fire of enthusiasm within an interested buyer in order to make a sale. Rather, I am describing a person comparable to a stock broker or securities salesman. There are a good many practitioners of investment trades of many types, invariably licensed by federal or state agency. Not so, the art consultant, notwithstanding the fact that a purchase may run into millions of dollars, or the profit (or loss) in five or six figures, at least when we talk about those sales which make headlines. But, art is a field generally far removed from the daily hustle and bustle. Most transactions are of minor financial importance. Like in the good old days—let's say the Gay Nineties—legislators and judges still say: let the buyer beware. The seller is almost expected to reap an excellent profit."

Cordier is another dealer-appraiser who does not like to speak of art as an investment, though he concluded that talk by agreeing that the "chances" are good the investment will be profitable. He adds, "The client just wants to get his investment advice free, which the appraiser cannot afford to give free; and therefore, if the client asks any questions at all, he will ask a dealer.

While the dealer is not a disinterested party in most instances, he can be right or wrong, just as an appraiser could be right or wrong."

The point is that the collector must find his investment advice where he might. Hawaii's Tim Morrow contends, along with many others, that "it would be nice if universities and museums would be more cooperative in helping the general public." Still, it is quite possible to get authentications at some institutions, though seldom can a collector ever get an appraisal from them.

Ruth Burns talks about levels of advice, and it is important that the collector understand the different sorts of advice he might glean from the varying sources. For example, the reputable dealer should be able to guarantee an item's authenticity and point the purchaser in the proper direction to find all pertinent research data. Association meetings or other gatherings of collectors should add to the store of knowledge. She cautions, "It isn't easy to find an expert because, actually, who or what is an expert? So many people with a smattering of knowledge think they are experts. There is no end to learning in any field, so an expert is really someone who knows more than you do and can prove it. Appraisals are an educated opinion."

Ames poses the question that quite clearly explains the buyer's uncertain purchase. "The dealer can guarantee the authenticity of an item, but who will guarantee its value?"

Yet finding people in whom to place a trust is necessary. For example, Margaret Hilmes says, "I have one client who bought extensively in the fields of paintings, bronzes, jades, and furniture and had never heard the term 'restrike' regarding bronzes." And that term hardly requires great knowledge. So it's important to cultivate appraisers and dealers, if the collector's less than well read. "An appraiser has friends in the trade who are sources of information in both wholesale and retail fields," says Thompson. "He could refer an investor to a good, reliable dealer and advise him on values offered. In my opinion it would be unethical to buy at wholesale prices and sell in competition to his dealer friends. He may only act in his professional capacity, not as a broker or a dealer. He cannot buy from a client items he has appraised but he may refer an investor to the client."

The question of investment advisers gets topically hot whenever collectibles outperform the stock and real-estate markets. The public likes to swarm to where the action is. Explains William J. Croker, general manager of *Collectors News* of Grundy Center, Iowa, "Possibly a comparison might be the situation six or seven years ago when a local over-the-counter stock such as Medtronic set the stock world on its ear and everybody wanted to get into the local over-the-counter issues in the hopes of instant gain. It doesn't work that way—in collectibles any more than stocks. If a person is going into collectibles with a prime consideration of investment potential, he has to be an expert personally for there are few equivalents of even the stock brokers to guide him."

The collector always has to worry about buying at a reasonable price, and on occasion he should seek out an appraiser or dealer to represent him at auctions, shows or on the open market. "Appraisers can attend auctions for clients and buy better because of their expertise and knowledge," says Morrow. "They would not be tempted to make a purchase because of their desire to own a piece instead of buying it at the 'right price.' " Adds book dealer Warren Howell, "The auction is one of the arenas in which a dealer should excell."

What's more, the collector should have added confidence with a reputable expert representing him, because that expert's reputation for shrewd and smart buying is also at stake.

Considering the collector's purpose is to buy for both pleasure and profit, the collector should realize that there are circumstances and markets where he should not seek to get better than retail prices, and where his opinion may be as valid as any adviser's. One example is the contemporary art market. Few budding artists make it big and of those who do command good prices for their works, few will see their art stand the test of time. Robert Kaller, a fine arts appraiser in Carmel, California, says the dealer and appraiser should help the collector select specific artists and their works of art, but that assistance should stop there. "There are, in fact, wholesale and retail price structures in this field," he says. "The only reason for a retail price structure is that it supports distribution and display of artists' work. The man who helps break it down in effect helps to destroy the apparatus for the distribution and display of artists' work and eventually destroys their livelihood."

Auctions—The Testing Ground

The huge popularity of auction houses with the public is a fairly new phenomenon. In the past decade they have flourished so dramatically that the number of auctioneers has more than doubled. Now, regardless of the field, auction sales account for nearly half of all transactions. In the San Francisco Bay area a series of classic car auctions drew tens of thousands of old-car buffs. Hundreds of the older automobiles were sold, including some that were knocked down for tens of thousands of dollars. In other cities, like the Washington, D.C., area, Persian and Oriental rug dealers hold weekly auctions, drawing hundreds of people.

These auctions are fun, but they are not the right market for the beginning collector-investor—not if he is truly interested in turning profits even in the long haul. "It's absurd for a person who has only a little knowledge and too much enthusiasm to enter the same arena as a professional dealer," says Frank Knight of *Collectors Weekly*. "That means the amateur would hope to do as well in an auction as someone who knows value, authenticity, and quality."

Yet these oft times emotional extravaganzas play an extremely important role in the education of the collector. For here there is the opportunity to closely study and compare pieces, to attempt to establish value before the auction. One thing that remains true, even in these days of large numbers of collectors, is that there is seldom just one item that will win your heart. Instead of buying an education at a too-expensive price through actively bidding at auctions, many experts counsel amateurs to silently pit their knowledge and desires against others active in the arena. A feel for value and quality can be gained, and cheaply.

More importantly, the auction house provides the best opportunity for the collector to personally handle a wide selection of items. Normally the show or display of items for an auction will be open to viewing for a day or two prior to the auction, and again the morning or afternoon preceding the auction. Often times similar pieces in a dealer's showroom already will have been restored, retouched, shined up, and generally given all of the cosmetic touches possible. On the auction floor, however, the auctioneer has neither the time nor the inclination to prepare individual items. His business is auctioning off items as they come to him, taking his percentage off the top of the sales price.

Robert Dalrymple of Ventura, California, an antiques appraiser, believes the pre-auction display and auction itself are among the best manners in which a person can prepare to be a serious collector. "The pieces are not always as represented, but the collector would be exposed to those that know and the collector will learn what the market is for the pieces that interest him." He says a person has to watch for late additions to auctions—items that were not on display prior to the auction—because they can be quite different than represented. Houston's Klep explains that auctions allow the collector to make price comparisons and to recognize quality craftsmanship. "The aim is to become able to distinguish a fine example of work by any particular artist from a good one, and a mediocre one from a bad one."

Auction sales are always final and there's no recourse after the gavel falls. Many of the best auction houses will draw up beautiful catalogues depicting and describing items; the auction house experts—and they are among the top authorities in their fields—will make studies of items and often establish their general value. Any work by the auction house, however, is to be used as a guideline only. At any auction the auctioneer makes repeated disclaimers that any item is guaranteed to be as represented, that the sale will be final, that the buyer is responsible for ascertaining the item's value. Still, many items possess a provenance and often times appraisers are called in by the person who is offering the item at auction. In dealing with items of great value, the seller is as concerned as the buyer in making certain no doubts as to authenticity or value linger.

Most experts believe that auction sales—taking a very average and very broad look at them—represent from 40 to about 80 per cent of any item's retail value. This, of course, gives dealers a markup and collectors a relative bargain, if the item can be bought at that kind of figure. But auctions have ways of gaining momentum. One auction of fine and rare wines in London somehow possessed so much pizzaz and steam that very nearly every bottle and case sold could have been purchased down the street at the retail store at a lesser price. On other occasions, if the weather is terrible or, perhaps, the moon full, auctions do not bring the prices they should.

Philatelist Herst views auctions as the crucial testing grounds. "Auction sales are the prime market and in an auction the dealer must compete with his own customer or other collectors," he says. "Nevertheless, with his superior knowledge of the market, he stands a good chance to win the stamp and the collector then ultimately must meet his price." And in that arrangement, though the collector pays more for the stamp, he at least possesses a guarantee to the stamp's authenticity—if he is purchasing from a reputable dealer who guarantees his wares to be as represented. Herst says that was the key to his early success and has been the hallmark of his dealership for more than 40 years.

He adds, "The stamps that are the best investments are those that are the most difficult to buy. Many stamps can be bought at wholesale and at appreciable discounts from retail, but because of their very availability, they invariably are poor investments . . . But many 'investment counselors' will not mention that to the sucker." And it is because of this fierce competition at auctions for the best items that the collector can feel content that a rare and beautiful stamp will always be in hot demand and will lead whatever price increases occur in his field of collecting. Still, the key problem for the amateur collector at these auctions is knowing what motivates the person bidding against him, and if he does not know value and authenticity himself, he can suddenly find himself in trouble. For example, a dealer may be readying a collection of certain stamps for sale and he needs one stamp to complete his showing. He can afford to pay a premium for the one stamp, if in so doing he increases the overall value of the entire collection by a much greater absolute figure.

Auctions can be manipulated, though the practice is not so common as it was at the turn of the century, both in this country and abroad. What was called a "ring" of dealers in a particular field would work together to hold down the prices of items coming on the block. This collusion worked admirably because members of the ring often constituted most of the dealers—and collectors on occasion—in the field. It was deftly practiced and the public bidding usually fell far short of what the true value of the item should have been. After the auction the ring's members would gather, often in a hotel room, to hold what amounted to a second but private auction. This time they would bid spiritedly against one another for items to sell to their clients or to stock their shops.

Before their private auction the ring would total up how much they had spent in purchasing items at the public auction. After the private auction amongst themselves, they would take another total, which would be higher, for it more nearly represented the true value of the items. The difference between what it cost them at the public auction and what they bid at their private auction would be the ring's profit. It would then be split between participating members.

This practice still exists—or so some experts claim, though hardly at such an organized level. The first to move to counter the ring's ability to stifle prices were the British, where the system of "reserve" prices was established. By law, the consignor of an item to auction could establish a reserve price. If his item was not bid up above the reserve level, the auctioneer would knock the item down to the house, eventually returning it to its owner. On such item's the auctioneer's percentage was lower. The reserve afforded the seller protections he had not enjoyed before.

But the reserve system soon developed its own abuses, many of which are still in use today. The reserve necessarily was a tightly held secret between the auctioneer and seller-consignor. Thus, it soon developed that dealers, artists, and collectors might consign an item with an unrealistic reserve price on it. The item would be knocked down at that price by the auctioneer, and there would always be a huge doubt as to whether the item in question had actually brought that price or whether the selling price merely represented the reserve.

Today, the reserve has been outlawed in certain states, including California where one of the two Sotheby-Parke-Bernet auction houses is located. Consequently, many of the major items to be auctioned off are sent to New York City where the unstated reserve system is still practiced. The reserve exists in California, to be sure, but it must be announced as one of the "conditions of sale." This comes of supreme importance because most appraisers and dealers away from the major auction houses follow the results of sales with an eagle eye, using them to establish value, trend and relative worth for other items. About 75 per cent of the appraisers, for example, agree that auction house sales prices are the best indicator of today's market.

Henry Cordier of Los Angeles talked of the pitfalls and dangers the collector faces, and for his speech he used graphics as an example, and he showed how what transpires at an auction can be most unsettling to even a respected authority such as himself. "When you consider graphics, there are so many factors which are of importance that the layman must rely on the experience and honesty of the seller . . . . The College Art Association may . . . come up with proposals to fight situations which frequently arise through the fact that many sellers do not routinely disclose certain facts about prints—facts which may substantially impair the prints' worth in the eyes of informed collectors. Would you know whether the image is a photo-mechanical reproduction of an art work; whether the image is a restrike or part of a posthumous edition; whether the authorized maximum number of artists' and other proofs exceeds 12 per cent of the number of prints in the limited edition; whether there are other authorized editions of the same image. While some dealers, not acquiring the prints firsthand, may honestly not know such details about a work, others may deliberately withhold such information to get a better price from an unwary buyer.

"I further find that positive authentication of graphics sometimes is a matter of luck. I had extreme difficulty obtaining agreement on a seemingly very genuine drawing by or attributed to Tiepolo, which after some hesitation I valued at $3,000. A few weeks later, I read in the *Los Angeles Times* that a Veronese drawing, identified by a single expert in Los Angeles, was sold at auction in Los Angeles for the amount of $57,500 to a major eastern museum. I must assume that the eastern museum knew more about this particular drawing than what made the news."

It is not that rarely that a museum gets stuck with bad buys either. Expert after expert talks of reproductions represented to be originals, of signatures added to works to increase their value tenfold, of restrikes, of genuine flim flam. To buy at auction is to be fully aware of the principle of *caveat emptor.*

Auction houses normally charge the consignor between 15 to 22 per cent of the selling price for their services. Most dealers, appraisers, and other experts agree that the good auction houses are both the best places to buy and sell. The auction houses stable of experts will establish generally what an item might bring, and it is a valuable service for the seller-consignor seeking to learn if a reserve price should be placed on his items and at what level. Yet, remember that none of the auction houses offer any kind of a guarantee of authenticity. An auction is the best example of *caveat emptor*. It's too late to attempt to authenticate an item after becoming the high bidder. Strangely, many appraisers say they spend as much time valuing items after purchase rather than before.

Here is where advice from a renowned dealer like Warren Howell is of inestimable help. "The auction floor is one of the dealer's homecourts. The dealer is—or should be—expert at purchasing at the right price. He should save the collector money." And he also then can offer his guarantee of authenticity.

Antique shows have small physical resemblance to the auction house, but the buyer needs to use the same amount of caution in making purchases at them. The shows are really a free-for-all; the wheeling and dealing is astonishing. At the San Francisco International Antique Show held at the posh and stately Sheraton Palace Hotel, 105 different dealers spread their wares. There was something for nearly everyone—antique jewelry, gems, glass imitations of gems, beautiful antique furniture, costume jewelry from Asia, old golf clubs, porcelains and assorted collectibles from old locks freshly gilded to authentic Chippendale chests.

The show runs four days, and then half of the dealers return to their shops locally and the other half packs its wares and moves on to the next show on the circuit. They have no shop, but move from show to show, much as the professional golfer or bowler moves along the tournament circuit. This is not a slur on these traveling dealers, but because they might be impossible to locate for fairly long stretches of time, and because they have no compelling reason to return to any particular city, the value of their guarantees does not carry the same weight as those of established local dealers. "Moving on from show to show really beats the problems of owning a shop," says Marty Flaherty, who with his wife runs Gramma's Attic. They live in North Hollywood, but have never owned a store. "The shop owner has that crime problem. It wouldn't be so bad if the thugs would just take the merchandise. But they always want to shoot somebody."

Flaherty's been on the circuit for nearly eight years, and it was his fifth time at this San Francisco show. "You build up a reputation," he says. "I guarantee that my stones are genuine, and I stand behind my sales." He's also an old hand at insuring his own sales. He was displaying about a half dozen aquamarine rings, and he acknowledged that aquamarine, next to the diamond, is the hottest stone. One other jeweler at the show had had an aquamarine ring so Flaherty paid about $150 for it, and then offered it for sale at $200. "There's no advantage to competition," he smiled. "I was at a show down South and another woman showed up with all of this nice gold work—chains and pendants and items like that. Her prices were terribly low so I went over and asked her what she wanted for everything she had. She told me, I bought it right then, and went on to have a marvelously profitable show."

Jeanne Coles represents the other kind of dealer who pays for booth space at such shows, most of which benefit charities. She has a chain of antique stores in the San Francisco area, one specializing in dolls and others in furniture. "Dealers do very nicely here," she says. "But yes, it's also a great place for the collector. If he has something to sell, he can bring it in and shop around, comparing offers. It's difficult to find another setting where you, any person with something to sell, can get 10 or 20 offers for your piece within an hour or two. The show officials and many dealers don't like it, because we pay for our booths. You can get around that by leaving it in your car and describing it to a dealer. If he's interested he'll go out and look at it. We dealers have to be as interested in buying right and getting new merchandise as in making a sale."

Flaherty was crowing over a purchase he had made

the previous day, not a sale. "This man I've bought a few things from in the past came to me while I was dealing with another customer. He took out this brooch and said he was in a hurry. He wanted $300 for it right then. I didn't even pick it up. I reached for my checkbook, wrote that baby as fast as I could and handed it to him. I had been reading this book at home that had brooches just like it in it.

"Look at this." It was a beautiful two-inch long cross that looked of Byzantium origin. The enamel work beautifully highlighted five sparkling red stones. "I'll bet that is a genuine 15th century brooch from Greece or Turkey. The stones have not been removed from their original settings, and the first reconstituted rubies were made in the 18th century. Those have to be genuine. If they are, it's worth probably $20,000. If they aren't, I still think the piece is worth $4,000 or $5,000."

Just then, a woman standing at Flaherty's counter asked him how much an aquamarine ring was, "That'll cost you $90," he replied, pausing a minute before adding, "That's what I paid for it and I'll just pass it along. It's glass; yep, I got stung." He says that no jeweler can tell the real colored stone from the synthetic without sophisticated equipment that's too costly for most dealers to own. "I take most of my stones to the Gemological Institute in Los Angeles to have the tests run. You can bet I'll have that brooch over there first thing after I get home."

It's also possible to ask other, uninterested dealers at the show to inspect items before purchasing them. Don't hope for a free appraisal of value, but it might take but a few minutes and fees are always negotiable—$5 or $10 should do it. And at these shows prices are nearly always negotiable. One dealer explains, "I figure out the competitive price, what I want for an item, and then mark it up another 10 per cent. It's a good idea because it always makes the buyer feel good if he is able to barter me down even a few dollars. Everyone wants to think they made a good buy."

In most instances the collector should exercise the

same caution at these shows as he does at auctions, flea markets and house sales. The dictum is buyer beware because there's no recourse, no one to go back to and say, "Lookit here, fella! This is not what you said it was and it is not what I thought I was paying so much money for. You even misspelled the name of the craftsman when you forged the signature."

Flim-Flam and Fakes

Only in the trafficking of narcotics and drugs do more dollars change hands fraudulently and illegally than in the world of rarities, objets d'art, and other collectibles. Most of Western civilization's priceless—ridiculously expensive, that is—art is so well catalogued that few collectors will make a major purchase without a provenance, a certificate of authority, a letter from the artist's dealer, a forensic text, carbon dating, microscopic and spectroscopic examination, or a museum curator's stamp. But there are levels of value and many collectors, for example, have houses full of antique furniture, some fine art, and heirlooms handed down from one generation to another and not one piece of all this will have papers, which hardly detracts from value. But it's because of these undocumented but authentic pieces that there can be so many undocumented, phony pieces.

Too, there's the obscure work of the famed artist or craftsman that was recently discovered—or created—and much of the art from eastern civilizations, Africa, and even the American Indian, all of which has never been catalogued. There are beautiful pieces that no one knows whence they came to be in a farmer's attic. The bargain-hunting collector can truly find fine items for a few dollars, but there may be just as many "bargains" that are nothing of the sort. Most dealers do not know authenticity nor how to establish it. Others do not care or deliberately pass an item off as possessing a much greater value. Perhaps the greatest pitfall for the collector is that posed by the shyster, the forged or faked item, and the flim-flam artist. "It's the person out looking for the miraculous bargain, who wants something for nothing that will get hurt or taken the most often," says Frank Knight.

Yet authorities contend that it is the item of marginal quality yet good value, say in the hundreds or few thousands of dollars, that are most often improperly represented. There's always a new scam. Whatever item suddenly becomes popular, the reproducers and forgers will soon be at work cranking it out in quantity. Appraisers are great skeptics. Houston's Tucker smiles slightly and says, "The only piece of art that you know to be authentic is the one that you watched the artist create." And obviously, that is impossible for the antique, which by definition must be 100 years of age. Tucker's point is that any item must be proved authentic, rather than proved to be other than advertised. It's important here to understand that there is no clear definition of what is a genuine piece, a fake, a forgery or a reproduction.

There are a myriad questions, none of which has been definitively determined by the courts or by the authorities within the different fields of collectibles. For example, it is a fraudulent act to sign a work of art by any name other than its creator, but is it a fraudulent act to expertly forge the signature of the artist on a genuine painting some great number of years later? Is that painting of less value? In furniture, where is the line between the restorer and the craftsman who in fact improves the piece's inherent quality and represents it to be of greater value than it was originally? In graphics, what if the print was not authorized but yet comes from the original artist's woodcut or plate, does that make that unauthorized print of less value than the authorized print, particularly when they are intrinsically identical?

The basic point is that the collector wants to pay for what he thinks he is buying. So the important distinction between fakes and forgeries and those pieces that are genuine reproductions, imitations or copies is in how the piece is represented. Some experts on early American furniture contend that the reproductions of the late 1800s are superior to the original Colonial pieces. But, still, these latter-day craftsmen worked with the same pride as their forefathers, and they did not attempt to pass their work off as century-old items. In the intervening years, some people have and others continue to.

The precise position the forger should hold in history and in the art market of today is difficult to define. Frank Arnau writes in *The Art of the Faker,* "The majority of forgers, and by no means the least gifted, practice their craft or trade—however one cares to describe it—for purely materialistic reasons. A perfectly forged Corot is easier to sell than a good genuine work by an unknown. The forger of real distinction stands head and shoulders above the commercial hacks of the international antiques racket. Intellectually and technically, he is a genuine artist—nor does he find himself in bad company. Michelangelo was not averse to dubious artifices. Rubens 'treated' other artists' paintings and executed copies to order. Andrea del Sarto was commissioned to paint a Raffaello Santi, now known as Raphael.

"Where does the copyist's work end and forger's begin? Why did such indubitably great artists lend themselves to such questionable practices? Was it a sympton of their lighthearted age or attributable to the homage they owed their noble patrons? If a duke or a cardinal sanctioned a fraud, did it cease to be one? Or was it only financial gain which lured the masters on? Forgery is at least five thousand years old . . . (but) the concept of 'forgery or plagiarism' is itself of comparatively recent date. It was not regarded as a punishable offense even as late as the Renaissance, although the counterfeiting of coins was a capital crime in pre-Christian times."

Not always do the fraudulent characters work to increase the value of an item. One faithful auction goer of the last century in New York City had a penchant for porcelain vases. He carried a common lead pencil with him, which over the years meant thousands of dollars to him. He had become very adroit at marking the neck or base of the vases he wanted with pencil-drawn lines that gave the vase the appearance of being badly marred. Invariably he would buy what was a perfectly beautiful vase much more cheaply than if he had not earmarked his property in the pre-auction show.

Many inexperienced collectors get preoccupations with the papers that provide documented value. "You have to realize that the provenance, the historical documentation of authenticity, is simpler to create than the forgery," says Lutton. "The swindler reads the same reference books as the bonafide expert and he knows precisely where the signature would have gone and precisely how to make that signature look like the real McCoy. He knows what people look for in attempting to determine the authentic items. Few of the early craftsmen signed their work, but you certainly can find many signatures these days." This holds true for furniture, art glass, cut glass, most of the fine works of the craftsman's art.

One of the problems that occurs when a collector discovers the painting he paid thousands of dollars for is not a Corot or Picasso is that he then must decide just how honest a man he is. Nearly everyone succumbs to the temptation at some point in life and it's not unlikely that many collectors have attempted to get out of a horrendous deal the same way they got into it. The collector has to pause when he considers the enormous numbers of faked paintings, graphics, pieces of furniture . . . the list goes on.

Richard H. Rush in *Art as an Investment,* writes, "Probably the most faked artist who ever lived was Corot. H.C. Marillier, the chronicler of Christie's auction house stated, 'America . . . was flooded to suffocation by Corots of doubtful ancestry. The legend goes that at one time they were being imported at the rate of four thousand a year. Corot may have reduced his system to a formula and been able to paint endless still pools with pale verdue in his studio, but he could scarcely have manufactured them in anything like such quantities as this.' The statement," adds Rush, "has been made that in his life Corot painted 2,000 pictures, 5,000 of which are in America." Rush adds that one French doctor who died in 1923 had accumulated 2,414 spurious Corots over the years from obscure dealers at low prices.

The case of the Dutchman van Meegeren that was discussed earlier shows the magnitude of the forger's art, when the art is perfected. In all, van Meegeren's forgeries of Vermeer and de Hooch totaled eight paintings that sold for $2,289,000, and remember those are World War II era dollars.

Arnau's *The Art of the Faker* is a fascinating book and he details the methods of the faker and forger in nearly all art forms, paintings, furniture, textiles, ceramics, printed works, sculptures, objets d'art. On furniture, Arnau is especially good. He writes:

"From the forger's point of view, there is scarcely a more lucrative or extensive field of operations than that of antique furniture. The wish to surround oneself with old furniture may often be prompted by a subconscious belief that fine old pieces provide unobtrusive but tangible evidence of family background and tradition. It is undeniable, too, that there emanates from the fine workmanship of old cupboards, heavy tables, solid chests and armchairs an aura of calm and dependability which is especially welcome to those who live amid the bustle of modern times. However, the demand for works of art by the cabinetmakers of past centuries can hardly be attributed to the aesthetic sense alone—not, in any case, where old pieces are acquired rather than inherited.

"The purchaser of any antique furniture, especially pieces of particular beauty or value (the two do not invariably go hand in hand), should ask himself to what degree they originated in the period to which they are ascribed. Certainly, no other province of art or craftsmanship includes a higher percentage of fakes and falsifications than that of old furniture. These include:

"(1) The complete fake, a piece of period furniture which looks old but has been newly built in its entirety. Copied by hand from an old original, often with consummate skill, carefully aged by specialists and apparently complete with all the characteristic features of old cabinetmaking, this is insinuated into the market as a piece of genuine antique furniture.

"(2) The professional or even industrial manufacture of period furniture from old wood.

"(3) The reconstruction of a dilapidated but genuine old piece using additional components, made of old or new wood, which are adapted to the original members and artificially aged.

"(4) The fraudulent embellishment of a plain antique, whether wholly or partially genuine, with inlay or ornamentation to simulate an appearance of greater value.

"(5) Falsification with the aid of genuine old stylistic elements, such as the addition of so-called 'noses' to unadorned Frankfurt cupboards. These and other forms of 'improvement' are used in order to disguise date and place of origin. A similar purpose is served by replacing the tops of commodes or tables with slabs of marble, for the age of a marble slab, especially if it has been skillfully treated, is extremely hard to establish."

It is easier to use a stamp reproduced in metal on a piece of furniture than to forge a signature to a painting. To forge a piece of furniture, photographs can be enlarged and exact proportions of the subject piece can be determined and then it is merely whether the cabinetmaker has sufficient skill. Or it is relatively simple to add the proper knocks and impressions, rubbed with a convincing manner to get the proper patina, to relatively new items. Other experts say it's important to check nails to see if they match the requirements of the period, the joiner work, and more.

These altered or faked items are not that unusual today. New Orlean's Cohen says that "unfortunately bad material is on the market in profusion. Many coins have been 'whizzed' (buffed highly) to enhance their value and unfortunately the neophytes bite on this because greed seems to prevail rather than good sense. Altered dates and just pure counterfeit coins are also on the market in profusion. Con games are becoming more prevalent. Unfortunately, physical theft of coins is a big factor too."

It's big in most fields. Morrow says, "You can date back as far as you want and you will find that the expertise of many artists has been able to duplicate most things of value. Burning, staining, coating, baking, burying, camouflaging, repairing, enhancing, dying, combining stands and glass cases, etc., to make items look authentic and important, are all methods of increasing the amount of money obtainable for an item."

The burn comes most often because a person wants to believe in miracles or because he is so willing to believe that he is getting the buy of the century that his eyes are glassy to any sound reasoning. Says John Klep, "The supply of suckers seems to be inexhaustible, as is the supply of sharks willing to take advantage of the suckers." Other experts say the flim-flam artist and the fraudulent representation, as Lyle Downey puts it, "are the usual rather than the exception." Adds Shreiber, "Some shops should advertise their place of business as 'Antiques and Fakes!' "

Nate Bradlin explains the pitfalls and dangers the buyer runs into when seeking out the expensive stringed instrument. "Many misguided or somewhat unethical repairmen and dealers are label switchers or fake label inserters," he says. "Many unlabeled instruments are sold to the advanced or not too sharp amateur violinists as 'in the opinion of the seller' as a fine 'French' or other famous makers work . . . Watch for the 'good-deal-under-the-market-value' seller."

Other fraudulent activities to watch for—incorrectly dated items with no substantiating data, the "instant antique" such as the rage recently with Wells Fargo Bank belt buckles, the huge amounts of expensive glassware created in France in the past 50 years, the 'antique' furniture continually turned out by the south-central European antique factories, and apocryphal marks on porcelains. Most experts also say that the too-often-used terminology, "can be attributed to the artist" or such, is often a red flag of caution.

The advertisements in newspapers or trade publications about "bulk lots" too often are a prime example. Seymour Freeman, the Arizona gemologist, says he has checked out the offers on bulk lots of diamonds. "They advertise them as being priced below the market. What market are they talking about? They prove to be, for the most part, about 20 per cent more expensive than regular retail prices."

The same is apparently true in many other fields. Herman Herst, the dean of philately experts who lives in Boca Raton, Florida, says it works a little differently with stamps. "A good example are the countries, which issue stamps primarily for collectors to buy, such as the Arab sultanates with 90 per cent illiteracy who issue stamps commemorating U.S. space exploits, in English, solely for this sucker market. So-called 'limited edition' first-day covers as advertised in the lay press are also prime examples. Overpriced, they are absolutely unsaleable."

People get in trouble when they start trying to beat the system. For example, the art dealer comes to town, takes a plush, impressive hotel suite, and advertises fine bargains. "I'm convinced that they salt most of those shows," says John Tucker of Houston. "There's no way a person can walk in off the street, listen to a spiel, and walk out with a good painting at a bargain price." And if the painting is not what it is represented to be, is the buyer going to track the dealer down in another hotel suite in another town? The field is wide open in nearly all collectibles. Truly, it is *caveat emptor.* A person can be sold a genuine Currier and Ives print with a bonafide provenance and still get hurt badly. For example, the dealer shows the buyer the recent auction sales prices where six or twelve similar Currier and Ives prints brought big sums. He then says that is about what this one should bring, but 'I'm obviously not asking that much for this one.' Watch out. Of the 7,000 Currier and Ives prints, only about 200 of them are regarded of great enough value to command the big price.

One of the best markets for the faker or forger is that for items which are extraordinarily easy to reproduce in a manner so that they possess that "instant-antique" quality. Among them might be the nautical running lights and lanterns produced in Hong Kong, the coal-oil lamps, often with imitation Tiffany-type shades, that have been such collector prizes when found at reasonable prices in the backcountry of California. Ms. Hilmes adds, "Recently 'old ivory carvings' have flooded the market. Some of these are even cast from some material vaguely resembling ivory. Too, brand new 'Ch'ien Lung' jades are selling for extravagant prices, having been sent directly from Hong Kong or Taiwan."

What compounds the confusion regarding the item that is represented to be authentic is that some of them possess intrinsic worth of their own. How, then, is the dealer to price this replica, copy, imitation of the original? After all, there's a growing market in the beautifully made stained glass by America's new crop of young artisans, much of it appearing to be of another era. Because it was made in America, does that give it worth and collectors' value? The answer is never simple, but buyer-collectors can never go too wrong if they follow the two most common pieces of advice, "Buy only when you know what you are buying and buy only what pleases you so much you really don't care if you ever sell it."

Investing—Or Speculating?

One Wells Fargo Bank vice president in San Francisco is fond of saying, "An investment should mean profit. A speculation can mean profit, but ordinarily a speculation is an investment gone sour."

We would all like to think of ourselves as investors rather than speculators. Webster's defines the verb speculate: "To enter in a transaction or venture the profits of which are conjectural or subject to chance; specifically, to buy or sell with the expectation of profiting by fluctuations in price." The dictionary defines the verb invest: "To lay out (money or capital) in business with the view of obtaining an income or profit; to convert into some form of wealth other than money, as securities or real estate, with the expectation of deriving income."

The difference in the two definitions of these uses of money turns on the words, "chance" and "expectation." There's a world of difference between them, and the collector must decide early which of the two best suits his financial circumstances and psychological makeup.

Just as in the world of the stock market, some collectibles are considered "blue chips" and some mean the buyer is truly "flying the kite of speculation." Margaret Hilmes expresses the common view of most experts regarding the well-established collectibles such as objets d'art, coins and gems, "I would compare investing in art with investing in real estate," she says. "In each case you hold something tangible. In each case, over the past 25 years, for example, the dollar value has increased greatly."

Says another dealer, "You don't hang stock certificates on your wall, nor do you take photographs or samples of the earth of all your real estate holdings and display them prominently. But you wear fine gems, you admire great paintings, you cherish eating off an antique table and drinking from fine crystal, and you possess great pride of ownership in items of beauty that tell the world of your impeccable taste. To me, that puts an investment in objets d'art far ahead of any other use of money, even though most collectibles have been outperforming the stock and real-estate markets for decades."

The great problem with collections as investments is that they are not liquid, and in fact, may at times require months or years to dispose of at the "right" price. Finding the right buyer for your item, it turns out, is many times more difficult than buying the item originally at a reasonable price. So the selling is as important as the buying if one hopes to realize what have been twofold increases in value recently for many items.

These days most people worry over what might happen to their investments in the event of another Depression reminiscent of the one of the 1930s, and as many more people worry about how to protect their capital against the eroding force of inflation. Collectibles, at least in the view of these admittedly biased experts, perform better than other investments in very nearly any economic climate.

For example, in the Depression some collectibles such as rare books lost immense value, though that deflating trend had started before the crash of 1929. Paintings fell in value, too. But, rare coins did not suffer greatly during the era, and began booming in 1934, gems maintained their value quite well, as did stamps. Says Frank I. Zoglin, a Kansas City appraiser, "During the Depression money was to be made in antiques. They didn't lose value as much as other items." Several appraisers and dealers who have studied price movements then concur that antiques lost about 15 per cent, possibly as much as 30 per cent during those bleak days.

These figures and estimates relate to fine antiques, and to the fine antiques that remained in vogue. The collectibles' market is hinged tightly to current taste, the craze. Richard H. Rush writes in his respected reference work, *Antiques as an Investment,* "Antiques were still booming to a certain extent well after the stock market crash. There is some evidence that antiques lag behind business conditions in general, both in the recession phase of the business cycle and in the recovery phase, and that they have a cycle which varies in length and amplitude from the general business cycle."

The years since Rush published his huge work in 1968 have served to corroborate his theory that antiques—indeed, nearly all collectibles—may react more to other factors than to the nation's business activity. Particularly for the individual collector, the message of Rush's book is that fashion, vogue, or popularity is of much more concern than the country's general economic health. He charts the rise and fall of French, Italian, English, and American antiques. He says the demand for these specific items is based on whether a style or a period of furniture is 'hot', rather than on the impact of wars, inflation, or recession.

This data reinforces the view that the collector with superior knowledge of the marketplace in his specialty will see and understand price movements better than the average dealer or neophyte collector. The correlation between values in collectibles and the general economic mood is not set firmly, though it is certainly true that in times when people have greater financial resources there is a greater inclination to turn to collecting. "People buy in the different areas of collecting in times of inflation to protect their capital," says one appraiser, "and they buy collectibles in times of recession to protect their capital."

It sounds paradoxical yet people collect for different reasons, and it is undeniably true that since World War II very few collectors have failed to turn fine profits. The true question is whether collecting in fact will remain the investment for all seasons, as it has been for the past 30 to 40 years. The answer is most likely that the value of collections will decrease as the fashion of the collectible and demand for it decline. In the case of the "craze" collectible such as nostalgia items and some contemporary art, the demand can be predictably set as enduring for only so many years. Remember the chart in Chapter Two that indicates the areas of collecting and the specific items that have peaked in value and now are declining somewhat.

This question of fashion or vogue is extremely important. Styles of antique furniture may have runs lasting for 30 or 40 years, then they will peak and it may be an even longer stretch of time before their value approximates in real dollars what it once had been. There is seldom a "crash" in collecting, but there are definite trends and once established, they gain momentum.

The market for any collectible has an intangible base. People want to buy this item for some reason and so long as there are continually more people wanting the item, then its value will increase. But it is important to keep in mind that value is based primarily on each item's quality and tastefulness—or, simply its desirability because of beauty, fashionableness, genius, or craftsmanship. And there are degrees of each of these virtues.

A Rembrandt will most certainly always be coveted by many art collectors, while the superb work of a Mendocino, California, seascape artist probably might never again be worth the $500 it originally cost the collector. It might but the odds are overwhelmingly against it. The same is true for coins. The beautiful, rare, unmarred coin in short supply will always have a buyer; the worn, common coin isn't even that desirable today with the millions of coin collectors.

The market for any collectible can collapse for many reasons. If the item is an old Coca-Cola advertising sign, a good argument could be made that it won't be worth hundreds of dollars when the current pop art-nostalgia craze passes. If it is common antique country furniture, a bust in the economic health of the country would probably drop the bottom out of that market. The wealthy people who are relatively unaffected by recessions do not collect country furniture; they collect early America, Italian, or French antiques, for example. The middle-class collector, though, who loses his job because his plant is laying off workers, will hardly continue to pay a premium for a table, vase, or beer bottle, no matter how old and rare.

That's the key to understanding this market—it is artificial in that taste and fashion change. For years there have been quality Victorian pieces of furniture that could be purchased for relatively few dollars. Fifteen years ago people were throwing out Tiffany lamps; then, last year one sold at auction for $35,000. What changed? It was not the inherent level of craftsmanship or genius involved in the creation of the item; it was the fashion. Today, for example, colored gems like aquamarine and turquoise are highly prized. Just five years ago they were trinkets. Or look at primitive art since Jackie Kennedy Onassis made it fashionable.

So when a person says that a collector's taste is all important, he is really saying, if the collector is interested in making a profit, that the collector's taste in selecting items that are fashionable is all important. The most successful collectors are those who spot the trends early or, luckily, had already become enamoured with items that suddenly became everyone else's craze.

Even in the fields that are fairly constant—rare books, coins, paintings by the old masters—taste fluctuates. The greatest profits could be made, for example, in rolls of coins this year, in commemorative coins next year, and possibly in silver dollars five years from now. Through all of those changes in fashion, the rare and beautiful coin will maintain its value and continue to advance in value too, but the speculator's chancy profit comes from spotting the movement in trends. For example, if a collector could foresee what national fad or interest follows the bicentennial fervor, he should become hugely successful.

It's crucial to remember that the idea of collections of coins, classic automobiles, or whatever as a fine investment is relatively new. As Reitlinger says, it has developed since World War II. Before then, the collectors were the rich and they didn't collect with profit foremost in mind. Today, however, the purchasing of collectibles itself is in vogue. It may persist for decades, and it is a reasonable belief because once great numbers of people are introduced to quality, beauty, and taste and seek it out, well, it's difficult to go back to modern bric-a-brac or some modern fashion based on today's synthetic materials and reliance on computers and machines. Still, remember that collecting by millions of people is a post World War II phenomenon and it comes because of the monies the growing middle-class and upper-middle-class have to spend, enjoy, and invest. That takes a healthy economy.

It has been said that buying right is the key to profits, but if that is true, then selling wrong can wipe out any paper profit. The early chapters have dealt primarily with buying, and indeed, it is the prerequisite. Too, if a person learns to purchase his items for his collection shrewdly, he should be able to sell as successfully as he buys. Yet, too often people get anxious, lose patience, and bail out. It's important to buy items that give great pleasure, for then it is easy for the collector to tell himself that waiting for his price is no burden, but instead affords the continual pleasure of owning a fine item. Too, it is important to build a collection. Indiscriminate buying is not nearly as effective as well-planned and extremely selective buying. In collecting coins, it can be a relatively simple process to know what constitutes a fine collection, but in other areas it is not so clear, and it requires as much study and contemplation as the actual hunt for specific items. After all, the pinnacle of collecting is the renowned collection, and as philatelist Herst says, the best items for a collection—and for investment—are those most difficult to find or to purchase because of the competition for them.

But with collectors whose status is less than that of

the wealthy, hugely experienced collector with the prized items in his collection, for which there's always a great demand, selling may not be quite so easy. There are, of course, many different ways and each has its own place.

Some of the markets are more adaptable to certain types of items. For example, the wide field of collecting includes such things as comic books, Depression glass, bottles, and railroad memorabilia. Many of these items are advertised in publications like the *Antique Trader* and the *Tri-State Trader,* which started in 1968 and now has a paid circulation of about 30,000. If the collector's item for sale is an expensive antique or objet d'art, he might be best off placing it in a shop on consignment.

Auction houses will place very nearly anything on the block, and if one house won't, another certainly will. There are the shows and exhibitions, flea markets and house sales. Always the seller should attempt to find the people who would most likely be interested in purchasing his collection. A good place to sell a set or collection of rare coins would be at a meeting of numismatists or at one of their conventions. It is possible, too, to make the round of dealers and get their offers for the coins.

Generally it is the beginning collector who wants to sell some early purchases who has the most trouble. As the quality and value of his collection increase, as his knowledge of his area of collecting expands, he will see where he buys his items and he will personally know many other collectors of similar items to his own. These people offer a prime market, and often the seller has little more to do than let it be known that his wonderful Stanley Steamer is available.

Here again the difference between speculation and investment can dictate the manner in which a collector can sell items. The speculator by definition is usually immersed in a fast-moving fad and has no intention of holding onto his collection for an indefinite period of time. He needs action to realize his profits and he will simultaneously advertise his collection, seek out other collectors, and frequent shows that include his particular items. The investor, however, has purchased his collection to hold over a period of years, selling only when he gets his price, when he decides it is time to upgrade his pieces.

And collectibles ordinarily offer tax advantages. Usually the only tax associated with them is capital gains, and many of the experts agree that valuable antiques, gems, or paintings are often used by many people to partially shield or hide assets. Also, many times an appraiser values an item for a collector who then donates the piece to an institution, using the capital gains as a write off. It is often as important to consult an accountant as to get top dollar if profits are to be maximized.

In collecting, another definition to separate the investment from the speculation could turn on the collector's level or degree of information or knowledge. Enough investigation and research could, after all, spell the difference between the "chance" of speculation and the "expectation" of investment. Or, that edge could come because of the advice of a respected dealer or an appraiser. It is the quest for knowledge, the process that leads to expertise that makes the difference.

Know What You Like

Collectors generally follow some strategy, even if it is illogical as my own when seeking antique furniture. But as happens so often in collecting the buyer can get lucky and I did, and in an innocent fashion my strategy was sound. I needed a side table, a dinner table, and some chairs. I knew little then of antique furniture, but I did know that it was appreciating in value where the modern manufacturer's models of plastic molded items lost a good 75 per cent of their value when you carried them out the door.

The dinner table I purchased gives a good lesson to both buyers and sellers. I had first spotted it in one of those small antique shops run out of a garage, and the woman was asking $250 for it. This was 1975, and she told me that if it were refinished it would be worth at least $600. It was a circa 1850 blond oak table about four and one-half feet square with five massive legs, though they didn't have the coveted lion's paw club feet. I kept thinking about that table and one day stopped in at her shop again. "I'm going ahead and refinishing the table," she said. "It'll cost you $350 as it stands now."

Time passes, about a month, and one day I notice an advertisement in the local weekly newspaper that she is selling all of her merchandise because she is going out of business. The next Saturday I stop by and ask her what has happened. Her health has been troubling her, she says, and her husband has told her to liquidate. I offer her $250 for the table, but she declines. Then a week later she calls me to say the table is mine at $250 if I want it. Six months later I have an appraiser to my house for the purpose of taking out an insurance fine-arts rider, and he values the table at $850, and offers me $650 for it.

I love the table, and I use it to write on. But there

are several lessons here. The woman who owned the small shop had to sell, and she discovered just how difficult it is to find the right buyer at the right time. I was fortunate someone else did not buy the table out from under me, but I also had indirectly established what the table was worth to me. I was the right and only buyer for the table so I received a bargain. She was the seller needing to liquidate and could find no other buyers. It is the greatest pitfall in collecting, spending too much for items and then finding that some emergency forces you to sell certain pieces.

The chairs also came to me as a gift. I went to an auction at the dis-establishment of the San Francisco Druid temple, and found myself to be one of the few bidders present. It was not a formal auction but more a garage or house sale. The chairs are quite fragile in appearance but sturdy beyond belief, as is usual for country American furniture. I paid $16 each for seven of them. Today, they are worth about $125 each, a nice profit in three years.

An even better bargain was my purchase of a brass ship's wheel, an 80-pound behemoth that I found at a Portland, Oregon, ship wrecking yard. I paid $35 for it in 1970. Two months ago I saw an identical wheel in Tiburon, California, for sale at a nautical antique shop for $399. The point is that the bargains are out there, though they are increasingly difficult to find. None of these purchases I made were meant to be investments, yet antiques have been performing so well that I have a $2,000 paper profit—it is only a profit if I can sell the items for top dollar.

I have friends who have purchased some of today's sleek manufacturer showcase furniture and are extremely proud of it. In talking with them, I discovered that they paid three times what I did for roughly the same furniture at about the same time I purchased mine. Today, however, my items are worth twice as much as theirs, easily.

Unknowingly at the time, my purchases followed one of collecting's best strategies. I was buying only what I truly liked and only that which I could handily afford. And luckily I was buying from people who did not know the market or had been forced into a corner where they were forced to sell below market value.

There are strategies for collecting and they pay off handsomely, particularly since the market generally keeps climbing. They are not so clearly stated nor so dogmatic as many of the strategies recommended for use in the stock market. For example, one school of stock-market experts says flatly that the investor should never sell when the stock is moving upwards but that if a stock ever falls 10 per cent from its high—sell right then. Others chart price-to-earnings ratios, selecting certain firms within industries they particularly like, and see huge profits coming because this certain outfit must outperform the market generally. Still others chart the rise and fall of the Dow Jones Industrial average, predicting subsequent market moves from their graphs. They then select companies to purchase and hold them so long as the chart looks as though the averages are still tending upwards.

The great advantage of securities over collectibles is the liquidity they inherently possess. If the owner of a stock or bond wants to sell, he need only call his stock broker to make the sale. And he can tell his broker at what price to sell—or buy. Often times he can get caught if the stock is either falling or rising rapidly, but even in those instances the purchase or sale can be made at the market, which is generally close to the price the investor had in mind.

With collectibles, the diversity of the market place, the element of luck in finding a buyer or seller, and the inherent differences between any two items make it absolutely impossible to determine a finite value from a distance. The item might be a fake or reproduction, it might be badly damaged—or in beautifully perfect condition, but the would-be buyer will not take the seller's word, unless he has done business with him before and knows that his word and opinion of value are impeccable.

So here is where the process of collecting becomes of huge importance. In the chapters that deal with appraisers, dealers, investment advisers, auctioneers, and flim-flam artists, the information has been presented to afford the collector a better understanding of how these professionals work, their fees and markups, of the services they offer, and of when to be wary of certain practices. Too, the collector has certain responsibilities to himself if he hopes to profit from his purchases.

Strategies must conform to circumstance. If the collector has thousands of dollars to put into a collection and feels that now is the time, his considerations will be of a far different nature from those of a collector who starts with a few hundred dollars—or less. The collectible itself will say much about strategy, because the guidelines change dramatically if the collector chooses to seek out paintings by old masters instead of Depression or carnival glass. Or a person may have bought an old Victorian home and is in the process of restoring it to its original condition. This involves a hunt for items of the period, and the restorer will hardly be able to become expert in all of the areas such as stained glass, intricate wood carvings, and other accouterments.

The next several chapters will take up individual areas of collecting. In examining antiques, gems, or coins, for example, the precise role of the different professionals and guidelines for when they should be utilized will be discussed. The amount and types of expertise and knowledge the collector should necessarily accumulate varies, too.

But after all, collecting for pleasure and profit can be as simple as purchasing genuine quality items at a reasonable price and, after a period of time if the market value increases as has been so true, selling at a fair price. Bargains are great, but the basis of a collection will not come from the rare finds. It will be built upon sensible, wise, and discriminating buys, which taken together create a collection of greater value than the total value of each item sold individually.

The collector needs to know why he is collecting, which is a more difficult determination than it at first must seem. If he collects purely for profit, he must be sure he never makes the "bad" purchase that can wipe out his entire profit for a year or even years. In this instance, he must invariably seek out second and third opinions of value and authenticity. What's more, he needs to keep a very close eye on the trends of market prices.

But if the collector views himself as a holder of a bit of antiquity, a bridge between generations of people, he will probably want to add to the sum of knowledge known about his collection. He'll want to become an expert himself, possibly a lecturer or author. Depending upon what he collects, he could view himself as an anthropologist-archaeologist. His collection will become very much a part of him, and he will probably become immersed in association meetings, research, and the frequenting of museums and libraries.

Or the collector may simply seek the pleasure of owning aged and beautiful items. Here again he will probably seek out all forms of information. His friends will see his collection as a reflection of his taste. His travels may become more involved with adding to his collection or in viewing other similar collections. There will be a richness to his life that may be of greater importance to him than the increasing value of his collection. And, of course, a collector always has the capability of turning his avocation into a profession.

So the collector has every reason to be exceedingly careful of the items he chooses to purchase. Inevitably, they will occupy a good part of his time. Some collectibles such as gems require formal study. Others, like country antiques, take more browsing, handling, and informal reading. In other words, the collector should select his field with the same care he uses in making his purchases. Now to specifics.

Diamonds and Other Gems

Rare and beautiful stones can be a fine investment if bought properly, but this area, as much as any other, requires the advice and assistance of the professional. "The diamond has the greatest value and the greatest sale," says Seymour Freeman, a jeweler, appraiser, and gemologist in Scottsdale, Arizona. "The world is diamond-oriented; we've been brainwashed into it."

Diamonds are always the best selling gems, but just this decade the colored stones have suddenly turned hot and today they are the rage. In 1972 aquamarine sold for about $20 a carat; by early 1976 top quality aquamarine was commanding $200 a carat. The craze was for turquoise before aquamarine began its run, but now the demand for turquoise is falling off. In 1975 pure turquoise cost $250 a pound and more, while "treated turquoise," an attractive, machine-made plastic imitation, costs from $6 to $20 a pound.

The treated turquoise looks so similar to the real thing that dealers and Indian jewelers have been fooled. But very nearly all colored gems can be doctored to enhance their color, appearance of purity, and general value. It takes a high degree of knowledge and sophisticated equipment to determine genuine stones from the fakes. In diamonds, the problem is compounded by the gradations, color, and imperfections inherently different from gem to gem.

Despite the beauty of the imitations, the bonafide gems have increased dramatically in value. Diamonds can be considered a fine investment, most experts agree, if they are bought at a good price, and the colored gems can be exceptionally grand speculations, if the collector doesn't get taken and reads the market right.

Freeman says the value of diamonds is tied to the international money market; if there is inflation anywhere in the world, the value of diamonds will reflect it. "There is absolutely no safe investment," he says, "but when a devaluation or depression occurs, the diamond is one of the very last things to lose value, and then it is always one of the very first to regain its value."

Since 1960 the value of the finest diamonds—the perfect one- to three-carat stones—has increased five times. In the two years ending 1974, diamonds increased in value by 250 per cent. In 1975, the increase was another 35 per cent. The first couple of years in the 1970s saw the increased demand from Japanese fueling the increasing values, and ever since the Middle East oil-producing countries quadrupled the price of oil, the greatest demand for diamonds has come from the wealthy in that part of the world.

In talking about diamond prices and values, the peg is the wholesale price structure, which is controlled by a true international cartel. It's essential for the diamond purchaser, if he is seeking profits, to buy wholesale because the jeweler's retail markups often are as much as 100 per cent.

Since the individual cannot buy at wholesale prices himself, the professional's ability is essential. Price is a good enough reason, to be sure, but there's just as compelling evidence that this field is fraught with pitfalls, with fakes, glass imitations, yags, and more. The dealer can assure the collector that he is getting what he pays for, that the dealer's reputation and expertise are the guarantee. Most gem appraisers say that the local downtown jeweler does not possess sophisticated enough knowledge to be that helpful. Raymond Fenster of Ray Jewelers and Appraisers in Brooklyn, New York, scoffs at the question, Can most dealers be regarded as responsible judges of an item's worth? "No! There are not many, and a person just has to look for them himself."

An unnoticed imperfection, or the misgrading of a diamond's color, can make as much as 50 per cent difference in a stone's value. Freeman says that the grading of a diamond's color is an exacting job, and one that is so demanding that he considers it necessary to return to the Gemological Institute every few years to insure that he does not lose sight of the standards. And the marvels of the technological age makes it much simpler these days to enhance the quality of stones. The deft touch of the craftsman yielding the laser beam can quite imperceptibly improve the appearance of a diamond, unless of course the inspection of the stone goes beyond the jeweler's loop or magnifying glass.

Gemology has developed in the past 50 years and its effect has been to stabilize the diamond and other rare gem markets. "Today I can appear in court and say beyond the shadow of doubt that this stone is a ruby or a diamond," says Freeman. "A whole new science was first developed in the 1930s, and today there's little chance that a person can just pick up the knowledge; it really takes formal schooling."

Although imitation stones abound, the Scottsdale jeweler says that there "never was a time in our business when a synthetic stone upset the market of the natural stones." The one exception, and it's not really an exception, came when cultured pearls were first produced. That development knocked the pegs out from under the natural pearl industry, an upset from which it has never recovered. And although there are beautifully formed synthetic rubies, the genuine stones are commanding huge prices, primarily because few quality stones are being mined or found these days. Strangely, one of the tests that is used to determine the synthetic from the genuine stone, actually dissolves the fake.

There are other pitfalls. For example, if the unknowing amateur finds a beautiful diamond, cut in the old European style, he must know that that stone must be graded in value by the size it would be when cut to the American, round brilliant style. "That is the standard of comparison, the measure of value," says Freeman.

Freeman says that it used to be possible to find bargains on particular stones in different parts of the world, but he says that today, particularly in diamonds, the market is so well-organized and structured that unusual bargains hardly exist. A shopper who flies to the diamond centers of Antwerp or Amsterdam, he says, will find prices about the same as in New York.

Other gems such as jade, emeralds, rubies, and opals can be good investments, but it is much harder to find a truly knowledgeable expert on each of them and their market is not so well defined and established. There are, of course, exceptionally expensive gems of nearly all colors. Some emeralds are worth more than equivalent diamonds. They are judged by their size, their color, their purity, and their life or fire, or, as it's known in the trade, "greenfire". What good is a stone without fire, emerald, ruby, or diamond?

Colombia in South America is the source of about 95 per cent of the world's emeralds, and though the government owns the biggest mines, they have been closed because of violence, corruption, and the interests of the black market. The mines are being worked, news reports say, but the emeralds find the market illicitly. Too, there are far more fake emeralds than the genuine stone. The imitations might be a piece of quartz dipped in green varnish, a piece of glass from a gingerale bottle, or even a piece of quartz with an emerald veneer. And without sophisticated knowledge and equipment, the fake can hardly be differentiated from the genuine.

Until recently turquoise was not valuable enough for it to pay to produce the imitation substitute. Yet its use has become so prevalent that New Mexico has outlawed the sale of the imitation turquoise when advertised as "Indian jewelry." Instead, it must be marketed as jewelry of "Indian-style" or "Indian design." Benny Atencio, former chairman of the All-Indian Pueblo Council at Albuquerque, says his organization is troubled "because the consumer may spend money on a product he thinks is genuine, but which is plastic." The problem doesn't stop with the dealer who represents the jewelry as genuine when it isn't; once a piece of imitation jewelry is passed off as the real thing, the misrepresentation gains credibility with time and belief. At some point, however, some owner of the item will find to his dismay that what he thought was worth so many dollars is actually worth about a tenth as much.

This imitation, plastic turquoise actually is extremely low-grade turquoise that is treated. All turquoise mines produce stone of varying degrees of quality; some is so chalky one can write with it on a blackboard. When it is treated for use in jewelry, heat and pressure impregnate colored plastic into it, simulating even the webbed lines or matrix that is highly prized in the genuine turquoise. After treatment, the soft turquoise hardens to about point 4 on the hardness scale (a diamond is 10). Pure turquoise, which requires only polishing by grinding and buffing, usually has a hardness quotient of 6 or 7, sometimes 8. There's nothing wrong with the sale of the treated turquoise; the rub comes when it is passed along as the more expensive genuine stone.

The collector, then, must exercise great caution. He must realize that in this field of collecting he cannot compete with the professional and, indeed, requires his assistance. Too, whether the collector seeks diamonds, sapphires, or emeralds, he must find the expert who can also give him access to the wholesale market. Normally, the appraiser-dealer will establish an arrangement whereby the collector pays say, 5 per cent, to the expert. That 5 per cent can represent big dollars when expensive stones are purchased, but it is a small and reasonable fee if the collector does not have to pay the huge retail markup. There is nothing wrong with using a dealer as a purchasing agent as most are highly reputable, but one gemologist says, "these jewelers have to trust their chain of supply. And whenever there's a chain like this working on acceptance of quality without routine proof, there's plenty of room for the collector to get stung."

The credentials of the professionals in this broad

field of gems, semiprecious stones, and jewelry are important. A senior member of the ASA, for example, must have withstood the rigors of a day-long examination by an ASA committee of his peers. While completion of the Gemological Institute's course is not mandatory, it certainly establishes an appraiser's or dealer's credentials. Basically, the ASA requires that level of knowledge before approving the advancement of an associate member to senior member status. "We turn down more applicants than we accept," says Freeman. All of which emphasizes the huge difference between the jeweler and the gemologist. Often the jeweler attempts to fulfill the more demanding role, but that will occur ordinarily when it is not his money and reputation at stake.

The jeweler's loop or glass, while truly enhancing the view deep into a stone, is not sufficient. Flaherty, the Hollywood dealer in antique jewelry, says each time he has an expensive stone he personally takes it to the Gemological Institute of America for an appraisal. "You get fooled too often," he smiles ruefully. "You see that beautiful aquamarine there. It's about 25 carats and would be worth a lot of money. I thought it was genuine, paid big dollars for it, and then later found out it was glass. Sure, I could try to pass it along just as the guy I bought from did. But the only thing I have in this business is my reputation so I'll eat that loss."

Too often a dealer will not tell his client to go after a second and a third appraisal of value, yet it's only reasonable if the gem is supposedly worth thousands of dollars. Gems often carry provenances, historical documents with finite, detailed descriptions. An appraiser's report on a specific gem should be detailed enough so that stone could be identified from amongst a jumble of similar looking stones. Gemology is now a science and the mere explanation that the stone is nearly perfect with exceptional color is hardly adequate.

It's certainly true that antique shops dealing in jewelry and gems have much better prices than the retail jeweler. But in the realm of gems the collector really should work very hard at insuring he doesn't place himself in the position of "buyer beware" without recourse to a refund if the gem is less than advertised. The collector's biggest mistakes will usually come when he thinks he is getting the rare bargain that won't wait for him to get an appraisal or to insist the dealer provide that documentation.

Because less money is involved in buying stones like turquoise, aquamarine, or tsavorite, the collector might tend to take a chance more often. Still, in very nearly all circumstances the collector will enhance the value of his purchase by at least the value of the appraiser's services, just because that item then has documented proof of authenticity. One approach for the collector would be to deal with a reputable local jeweler, using him as an adviser and purchasing agent, but also using him to get appraisals and documentation for each item.

And in collecting gems, the role of fashion and fad plays a huge part. These days, because the price of the larger diamonds has skyrocketed into the thousands of dollars, jewelers are pushing exquisitely set clusters of small diamonds. None of the gems will be more than a quarter carat and though these flakes are beautiful none carry great value. The value of such a ring or brooch will stand almost entirely upon the genius, workmanship, and beauty of the setting, which is not the kind of speculative adventure the collector should engage in. He's much better off buying authenticated antique jewelry, which has an established and increasing value that's still probably less than the value of the newly created item. The purchase of the cluster of small pieces falls in the same arena as the purchase of contemporary art. What, after all, is the collector's probability of choosing the one artist in a hundred whose work will have lasting value? Slim to none at all.

Rare Coins

"A rare coin is like a rare painting in that its value is based on an increasing demand in the future," says Q. David Bowers, a leading dealer-auctioneer of rare coins. "I'm sure the demand will grow because coins are the ideal hobby-investment. With more people getting more leisure time, and if they continue to have discretionary money, the number of coin collectors must grow."

An investment must have a track record and coins have been traded for centuries, observes Frank Knight, a rare-coin appraiser before he began the *Collectors Weekly* in Kermit, Texas. "Since the late 1950s the number of coin collectors has skyrocketed and so has the value of coins," he says. "Sure, there have been hills and valleys in the movement of coin prices, but significantly the most recent valley is very nearly always higher than the one that preceded it.

"A person should be a collector before he becomes an investor," adds Knight. "It would be a good idea for a person to read, study, and compare many coins before buying heavily. Knowledge is value in collecting and the investor must realize he doesn't have even the protections he enjoys in the stock market, which are not protections for the foolhardy." That chief protection in the stock market for the investor is the knowledge that when he contacts his broker to purchase 100 shares of General Motors, he knows that he is buying General Motors stock and not some imitation certificates.

Before discussing in detail the various ways in which the collector might pursue an accumulation of rare coins, let's examine the market. Though it has suffered occasional weaknesses, ever since about 1934 the value of most rare coins has gone almost straight up. "Early in the Depression," says numismatist James H. Cohen of New Orleans, "some rare coins were selling so close to face value that it was ridiculous. Only excessively rare coins were bringing any type of premium whatsoever."

Bowers says it was the first price guide to U.S. coins, published for the year 1934, that created a surge in price and value. That handbook has been published annually since then and has sold millions of copies and is one of the top ten best-selling books in U.S. history. The Los Angeles auctioneer adds that an investment of $1,000 in quality rare coins in 1948 would have been worth about $30,000 in 1974. The increases in value have not only occurred for the old coins. For example, a roll of some 1960 pennies has increased in value about 10 times since 1964.

In mid-December 1975 the Bowers & Ruddy Galleries in Los Angeles auctioned off the Kensington collection and other rare coins for more than $1 million. *Coin World* reported, "Auction records were smashed in many series, new price trends were established, and proof was given of the strength of the coin market as a whole." It was a significant report because many experts had felt the coin market was softening. The highlight of the auction was the sale of early United States proof sets. There were 26 sets that had been offered at auction by Lester Merkin in 1968, and the value of these sets as realized at the Bowers & Ruddy auction had increased by an average of 151 per cent. "Not every set made that type of gain, though none declined in price. Many of the sets tripled in price over the period, some doubled, and others took more modest advances. Each, nonetheless, has proven itself over time as a worthy investment, representative on an active coin market," the report said.

More so than any other collectible, rare coins have been ballyhooed as a strong investment vehicle in the past few years. There is, of course, substantiating data in terms of price movements, but it is important to remember that coins, like other collectibles, derive their huge values because of the supply and demand ratio, and because it is fashionable these days to collect them. There is a book value to a coin—like a stock—but where the coin has a face value of perhaps 25 cents or $1 in the case of some that might bring more than $10,000, the stock ordinarily has a book value that at times approaches its selling price and a price-to-earnings ratio that can serve—again at times—to keep its value somewhat within reason. The coin market will remain strong so long as there are increasing numbers of collectors with money to spend on them, and it is certain, as many experts say, "the best of the rare" will always perform better than the more common items.

Today rare coins can only be obtained by buying them at auction or through dealers; the day when you could find the Indian-head penny or any pre-World War II coin in your change is past. Even so, the inevitable pitfalls await the unsuspecting. Counterfeiting, date alteration, coins that have been worn smoother than advertised or have been "whizzed" up by a dealer can trap the unsuspecting. Again, the collector-investor must first check the reliability of the dealer he utilizes.

The neophyte or uninitiated collector may have his problems early on. "In any field a man with special expertise and knowledge will probably come out better than the neophyte who merely steps in and buys because he has money," says Cohen. "It is entirely possible, of course, for a retail client to make money on his purchases providing he is fortunate enough to be able to pick coins that will be in demand on a short-range basis. If the dealer were positive of how to do this he would not need small retail clients to become very wealthy."

Cohen adds that not all dealers are that good at recommending purchases. "There are proficient pros, but it's not always easy to find expert guidance because, unfortunately, anyone can call himself an expert without challenge on the city, state, or Federal level."

Yet in coin collecting, there are several places the less-than-knowledgeable collector can turn to check credentials and reputations of dealers. The Professional Numismatists Guild and the International Association of

Professional Numismatists provide reference services, and both attempt in a limited manner to allow only qualified dealers in as members. And again, members and particularly senior members who have undergone the qualifying examination of the ASA are often good sources of information. Also, the American Numismatists Association Certificate Service (ANACS) will guarantee authenticity for a reasonable fee. Yet numismatics is a field that has grown hugely in the past few years, and the number of dealers has more than doubled, which is not to say the number of qualified experts has doubled.

Catherine Bullowa, a Philadelphia numismatics appraiser-dealer, says, "Sorry to say there are not too many people expert enough in this vast field, but we do have some good appraisers who can give excellent guidance if the collector will go to the pains of searching them out." She believes that the collector is best off first determining who is the most reliable and reputable dealer locally. "Then go to him and talk over the entire situation—the reasons for your interest, your finances, and your aims."

But she, like all of the other experts, contends there is no substitute for the collector's own expertise. "The only way to learn numismatics," says Cohen, "is to obtain and study as many books on the subject—supplement that with practical experience and wherever possible 'pick the brains of other numismatists.'" He adds that after the collector has learned the coin business to some extent, "he has to use his own ability coupled with that of a reputable dealer to determine a good price for any purchase." He says the different authenticating services should be used, the dealer's credentials and reputation checked, and that outside appraisers should be called in whenever there is any doubt regarding value or authenticity and when the amount of money involved is great enough to warrant the appraiser's fee. These appraisers can also be excellent investment advisers, "provided there is no conflict of interest," he adds. In fact, investment advisers abound, whether they be extremely well established and highly thought of dealers-auctioneers such as Bowers or just-established fast-buck artists with a huge advertising budget.

Bowers & Ruddy Galleries have become a subsidiary of General Mills, which by itself is not that significant, other than to reflect the fact a huge corporation sees continual profit in coins. Still, the auction house has continued to be more the personal effort of the two men. They offer a number of "collection investment programs" and though the results they have experienced may not be superior to other reputable programs offered by dealers, the terms are instructive. "Bowers and Ruddy Galleries, Inc., absolutely guarantees the quality and value of each item sold . . . . Here is what we guarantee," the promotional advertisement says. "We guarantee that you will find our grading to be accurate and the price paid to be reasonable. After receiving your coins you have seven full days to consider the coins, examine them, have them appraised by others, and to consider them in any other way that you wish. If, for any reason whatsoever, you are not 100 per cent delighted, your money will be refunded in full as per our guarantee. There is no red tape. In fact, no explanation is necessary."

Bowers & Ruddy offer several collections programs: a general selection of U.S. coins of various series, gold coins, silver dollars, coins of the world. Most of the programs revolve around the investor paying from $100 to $5,000 each month for his coins. Basically, the purchaser is selecting the auction house to buy for him which means he's paying about 20 per cent for the guarantee of value and authenticity. The guarantee of value, however, says nothing about future performance so the value of his collection still rests on an immense number of imponderables. The basis for investing in this type of program is the firm belief that the overall coin market will continue to advance strongly over the years.

Yet, coins come into fashion and fall out of taste just as readily as items in other areas of collecting. Ever since the U.S. government lifted its ceiling on the price of gold, rare gold coins have been in great demand. Too, silver dollars continue to be popular and in the wake of the bicentennial fervor, there's even more interest in other U.S. commemorative coins, such as Columbian half dollars of 1892 and the Washington-Carver issues of the 1950s.

Today, most experts agree that the early proof sets of U.S. coins will continue to be "hot" items. Most also agree that the rare coins from other countries will grow in value faster than most similarly rare U.S. coins. At other times, rolls of coins have been the vogue. Undoubtedly, if a collector buys only the coins of which there are only a dozen or so in existence, his chances of increasing the value of his collection become much greater. In coins especially, "the best of the rare" is certainly true. For example, there were many Roman coins minted and not only were they common in their day, they remain common and inexpensive today.

So the best advice to the collector is to work at gaining his own knowledge and then, with that as a starting point, go to other experts for advice and appraisals. Knowledge can come from many places. In most locales, the coin clubs and associations are extremely active and more often than not other collectors can be among the best sources of information. There are unlimited numbers of books and periodicals. They detail trends, price movements, unusual events in the coin world, and generally a good jumping off point from which the collector can start accumulating more detailed information. Don't be stingy in buying data; it pays for itself many times over.

In numismatics—the study of coin and paper money—the actual handling of coins, the study of the different issues, the knowing as to whether the buffalo nickel is of the raised ground variety, all adds up to confidence and eventual profit. Counterfeiting has always been rampant and it is today. Dates are often altered by experts so that it takes a fine, knowing eye to detect the differences. And many less than reputable dealers and collectors "whizz" or buff up coins in an attempt to move them up one graduation higher.

And that's the most important area—the grading of

a coin: Whether it is in fine or good condition, whether it is actually uncirculated. Even when the attempt at increasing the value of a coin is not deliberate, it occurs. Says Cohen, "Various auction sales, such as Stack's, tend to place values on coins, however, one must be adept at reading between the lines and knowing the difference between true top quality material and that of 'sliders' that just are not worth the same price."

There are several ways in which a collector can sell coins. One is to make the rounds of various dealers and get their offers. The seller will normally be disappointed as the dealer will be looking to tack his own profit onto the value he gives the seller. When the dealer buys wholesale lots of coins, he usually has room for a markup; when he buys from the individual he insures that he will have that markup.

Of course, advertisements can be placed in periodicals, the coins can be taken to numismatists' meetings, shows, and conventions. Or, the coins can be placed with one of the auction houses. Again using Bowers & Ruddy as the example, they accept no less than a $2,000 consignment. Yet auction houses are often where the most can be gained for a collection. Says Bowers, "When Armand Champa, one of America's leading numismatists, considered selling his coins he solicited cash offers from leading dealers. Growing dissatisfied with the time needed and patience needed to show the coins to many possible buyers and also feeling that the price was not right, he consigned his collection to us for auction. The sale was held and created worldwide attention. Armand Champa subsequently was so pleased that completely unsolicited by us he purchased ads in *Coin World, Numismatic News, The Numismatist,* and other publications to thank us for the job we did for him—and to state that his coins sold at auction for more than twice the highest price he had been able to obtain by soliciting cash offers earlier."

That is important—more than twice the money he was offered by dealers. This also holds true in other fields. Naturally, the collector must have a fairly representative collection to place on the block. Auctions are probably both the best place to buy and sell—if a collector knows the trade. It is also the easiest place to get hurt. As Frank Knight says, "Knowledge equals profit."

Stringed Instruments

Of all the areas of collecting, stringed instruments might seem unlikely purchases for investments. Yet the collector who has specialized in purchasing them during the past 2, 5, or 10 years has realized enormous profits. "Most good instruments of value have doubled and tripled in price in the last five years," says Nate Bradlin, the master violin maker, repairer, appraiser, and dealer.

"A collector can profit from retail purchases," he says. "In January 1973, a friend purchased an 1845 J.F. Pressenda violin at auction, retail value at the time, $8,500. This, like many fine violins is worth today (1975), because of its very good condition and tone, from $13,-000 to $14,000."

Bradlin says this increase in value has hit the price of new instruments, too. Even the cheap plywood and factory made instruments have skyrocketed in price in the past two years. Any instrument from a good maker, authenticated with papers, is an excellent purchase for investment purposes today and will become an even better investment in the future, as the supply of these fine instruments gets even tighter. "Speculation on these purchases is like putting money in the bank at the highest interest for your best return, which really is not speculation, is it?" says Bradlin. Adds Lyle Downey, another appraiser of stringed instruments who lives in California, "There is likely no 'true' peak in value. Luck, can help, of course, because it helps to be at the right place at the right time. But I believe that nothing is truly impossible in this area."

Historically, violins, cellos and other stringed instruments have been fine buys. The market has always been strong for the instrument made by the masters like Stradivarius, yet the common instruments of another century are hardly common today. Prices generally peaked in the early 1920s, fell off a bit in the late 1920s and early 1930s—though it was not a dramatic bust—and then during World War II and just after climbed to ten times the value they had commanded just 20 years earlier when the market had weakened. A good example, says Bradlin, are "most of the Carlo Antonio Testore instruments. Compared to Stradivarius, Bergonza, and Guarnerius Del Gesu, they were crude and very cheap but still of good tone. And because of their excellent tone they started to climb up in price in the 1920s and today, depending upon age, tone, and condition, go from $10,000 to $20,000."

There are very good reasons for these price increases in the field. Bradlin explains, "The popularity of the violin is showing forth. Some schools that teach music today are making the knowledge of simple playing a must. Many schools, on the lower levels, have been fantastically successful with the 'Suzuki' method of teaching and playing. There are many parents who learn along with their children."

Interestingly, the experts of the stringed instrument field believe that a big move upward in price is just now gaining steam. "Rare items appreciate in value far more than common ones," says Downey. "For example, a recently sold cello bow was bought for $75 and sold with ease shortly after for $400. Certain items, fine instruments and fine violin and cello bows are in very scarce supply." He adds that the cheaper instruments are not good items for a collector to buy for either speculation or investment. A collector should also be extremely wary of the "good deal" where he's offered an instrument under the market price. There are, of course, many of the practices of forgers and shysters at work in this field too. You'll possibly see fake labels inserted, the switching of labels, and the passing off of so-so instruments for those of great value.

And the huge question remains as to who is a responsible judge of value? "Only a crafted maker who has studied the art and who has followed closely the international and national markets for good instruments. He must be involved daily," says Bradlin. "Many fine music dealers are some of our best customers." As in many fields, it is the knowledgeable dealer who most often turns to the true expert for appraisals and information. "It is, of course, up to the buyer to decide when to call in a professional appraiser. If the buyer finds in his own mind the slightest reason for doubt, for *any* reason, he should get another opinion; especially if the buyer is considering a rather expensive or moderately expensive instrument from a private seller or other than from a known and reputable dealer."

Most astute buyers demand an authenticated bill of sale and accompanying certificates of appraisal and any other documents that help establish the instrument's provenance. If several hundred or thousand dollars are to be spent, the fee of, say, a couple appraisers is like adding value to the instrument. If and when it is to be sold, those appraisals create added value, because authentication has much to do with price.

The buyer should contact an expert before he considers buying any truly expensive instrument. He should strike a preset agreement with him regarding his fee, which might range from 5 to 20 per cent of the instrument's value. This adviser, however, can be asked to assume many roles—such as that of teacher, counselor, confidant, or seeker of fine buys. When he does make the purchase he should have the specific certificates fully spelling out the instrument's circa, school, condition, or precisely what it represents "in the opinion" of his expert, which may only be able to say it's "in the style of" or "can be attributed to" a certain school. It isn't unusual, either, for the buyer to be able to take an instrument out on a trial period to determine both whether other experts value it similarly and to play it.

These instruments frequently show up on the auction block. Bradlin says that often at auction one particular collector "doesn't want another bidder to have the instrument; hence, unrealistic prices are reached. Of the few rare masters that turn up for sale from time to time, away from the Philadelphia, New York, and Boston areas, you find that our midwestern appraisals are often more moderate. At some of the auction houses of New York and especially London you will find affluent collectors 'bidding up' to . . . at times very unrealistically high prices.'' The point, naturally, is that value cannot be taken off the records of these highly esteemed auction house sales. Here again, it is experience and knowledge that count. It is the expert who knows an instrument and its value and can say that sale should have been at a different price.

To be sure, the collecting of stringed instruments is not for everyone. Yet this field dramatically points out just how important it is for the collector to specialize, to limit his purchases to an area where he can accumulate knowledge. It is only smart business to rely on the field's top experts, and in very nearly every major city there is a knowledgeable expert, in this instance, of stringed instruments. ''You will find the knowledgeable appraiser-dealer-repairman is the person who is really making out well these days,'' says Bradlin. And there's no reason for the collector not to gain that same insight and data from him. Says Downey, ''The collector needs the aid of the appraiser or dealer who knows an instrument's true value, who will share his knowledge—for a fee—and who also does not stand to profit from the deal.''

Furniture—
And Caveats

Antiques and collectibles include everything from aged kitchen sinks to steam-driven clocks and magnificent Sheraton four-drawer chests. "We don't even use the word antique any more," says Alex Sabbadini, an appraiser who runs an estate-auction house in Sacramento. "But whatever you want to call the older items, they just keep shooting up in value. I was thinking a year or so ago that there had to be a ceiling somewhere, but now I'm not sure."

The boom seems to just keep right on building. Jeanne Coles, who owns half-a-dozen shops in the San Francisco Bay area, says that demand and price increases slowed for nearly a year, but then in the summer of 1975 prices started skyrocketing again. "A roll-top desk that would have been worth $450 in early 1975 is worth between $700 and $800 a year later." Frank Knight, the publisher of *Collectors' Weekly* in Kermit, Texas, illustrates the fields growth by explaining that 30 per cent of all the thousands of antique dealers nationwide have been in business less than three or four years. "On Stateline Street in Kansas City, 18 shops opened up within a two-year period," he says.

The appreciation in prices is not true of all antiques or collectibles. Knight figures that antique values generally have not advanced any faster than the rate of inflation. "Collectors are like sheep—they all want what is popular." And so again it is the story of the demand being greatest for that item that is in vogue, in fashion. The big money comes when the collector gets out ahead of a fad. Remember the tale of the Morans of San Antonio, who bought their Depression glass for a nickel or a dime apiece and saw it zoom to $5 to $15 apiece.

The difference between the collector and the profit-making investor is knowledge. "In glasswork, Tiffany has had many imitators, and they just keep right on making electric needles," says Moran. "For $2.50 you can take a fine piece of glass and turn it into a Louis Comfort Tiffany quite easily." But even with that kind of fakery and forgery, and even with the sure knowledge that the purchase is a Tiffany, there's little certainty that value will always remain so high. For example, 15 years ago Tiffany lamps were being tossed away—there were no buyers. Today, some Tiffany work commands tens of thousands of dollars. "Never before has it been so important for antique hunters to know the true value of the pieces for sale in shops and shows," says Ralph Kovel, who with his wife, Terry, are among the nation's best-known writers and lecturers on antiques. "It's not that antique dealers are less honest than other businessmen," adds Kovel. "On the contrary, the ethical level in the trade has traditionally been high. But the antiques boom has brought a lot of amateur dealers into the market, and many of these dealers don't know much about what they're selling."

To help avoid the risk of antique buying, the Kovels compiled a list of 10 caveats for the *National Observer:*

—You can only buy a bargain if you know more than the dealer. Study.

—Beware of reproductions, especially glass, the easiest antique to copy.

—Beware of the never-was "antique" that was made for today's gift shop. Ash trays of early styles of glass, milk glass, Mason jars, and cast-iron miniatures are just a few of the pseudo-antiques found at many shops.

—When buying furniture, be careful not to get a piece that is married (two unrelated pieces joined together, such as a table and a high-boy top), glorified (extra carving added), or a reproduction.

—Ignore the family history of historic-personage

associations. Believe only verified documents attesting to ownerships and history.

—Check for repairs, breaks, repaints, and missing parts. A black light will show many of these.

—Watch out for phony labels and signatures. Faked signatures etched into glass and paper-makers' labels are becoming more common.

—If you fall in love with an antique you don't know about, pay what a similar new piece would be worth to you. You can never overspend if you consider the use only as a yardstick to value.

—Watch out for fads. At times certain types of antiques are in top demand, commanding top prices. Then the fad fades, and the antique's value fades with it.

—Remember that antiques do not improve with age. If it wasn't pretty when it was new, it never will be.

Not all items just keep zooming upwards. The collectors' plates have boomed, but this year one Royal Doulton plate that had been valued at $125 a year ago sold for only $47. The collectibles—plates, glass, spoons, to name three—are true speculations where huge profits and substantial losses can be realized. The collector has to watch these price trends closely, because it often can take a longer period of time to sell items than he would expect or desire.

It is of great importance to differentiate between the true antiques and the collectibles, many of which collectors and dealers alike call antiques. The U.S. Government, for customs purposes, recently changed its definition of an antique from any item made prior to 1830 to any item now at least 100 years old. There is no import duty on antiques. Nevertheless, some dealers remain purists. Says E.R. Wilkerson of Atlanta, "My firm is only interested in antiques produced before 1830." That's an important date to dealers and collectors because machines then first started to replace the handmade furniture.

Most experts agree that the true antiques will always be in demand and that, even in times of economic stress, will hold their value. "Items can be expected to hold or increase their value (in nearly all economic climates) if made before 1790, whether of American, French, English, Russian origin, and most especially if they have desirable attributes of beauty of line, top material, and obvious craftsmanship," says George Manley, a Connecticut appraiser.

Generally speaking, inflation does not increase the value of items, and recession does not change their value either; the changes in value come because of an increase in demand, diminished supply, or because the item is of the fashion. "Depression allows for buying at low prices, but value does not depreciate in quality antiques," says one appraiser. He adds that good new furniture is expensive while good antique furniture is often not quite so dear. The important point is that good wood furniture greatly appreciates because of the scarcity of wood and the craftsmanship. Too, fine glass items such as those by Tiffany or Steuben greatly appreciate in nearly any economic clime because of artistic qualities, the breakage of some items, the fine materials, and the fine craftsmanship that will never be successfully reproduced.

Adds Ronald Schwarz, a San Francisco dealer-appraiser, "Historically, it has been shown that antiques and objects of art have held their value and increased in value even in times of economic stress." Most of these experts stress this virtue of fine antiques. Yet fashion is many times the dictating factor in regard to any item's value. Louis XVI antique furniture has been soft and the demand for it slow. There have been generations when certain eras of fine antiques never did enjoy popularity. Today, for example, Victoriana is making its first major comeback since the popularity it enjoyed when *a la mode*. Says an appraiser, "Remember that all changes in style have been precipitated by historical events such as wars, pestilence, economic booms, depressions."

The furniture market explains price appreciation, growing demand, pitfalls, rewards, and the new breed of collector. "If you spend $125 on a Victorian lamp table, you will probably get $150 for it a year later if you have to move and unload your possessions," says Sabbadini. "If you had spent the $125 on a new Swedish style table, you would probably be left with a used item worth about $20 or $25."

Dealers and appraisers across the country concur that much of the enthusiasm that creates today's boom comes from the huge numbers of young people and newlyweds who combine their limited budgets with a distasteful view of the modern "plastic" creations of manufacturers to see antiques as their first choice. It's not unusual for a young couple to spring for a brass bed—immortalized by singer Bob Dylan—and cough up $500. Before this current upsurge of interest in antique furniture, among the younger folks that dates from the mid to late 1960s, old brass beds would sell for $25 or $50, and old iceboxes could not be given away. Today the iceboxes command a couple of hundred dollars and are used for bars, stereo cabinets, or any number of storage purposes. Many of these items are not antiques by strict definition since they were made this century. Brass beds, for example, were not produced until the early 1900s.

The fad value of many items means it can soar in price almost over night. The nostalgia kick has pushed up prices on certain items more than 10 times in the past five years. The early Coca Cola advertising signs can bring as much as $1,000 now. If the collector spots the fad, whether in furniture or tin cans, radios, and bottles, big money can be made quickly.

Even copies of genuine antique furniture can be valuable. William Lutton, the San Francisco appraiser of French antiques, says that some of the finest Louis XIV and Louis XV pieces are worth as much as $30,000 today, "so most of the furniture you will see out of museums will be 'in the style of' or 'in the manner of' French antique. Many of the forgeries are better than the originals anyway. The emphasis placed on signatures on a piece seems absurd." What's more, he says few of the craftsmen who produced the beautiful and graceful French antiques signed their pieces. The signatures were either properly or improperly added later. "It's easier to forge a signature than to forge a piece of furniture," he says smiling.

He says that many people are collecting furniture to give them instant heritage. "I think that it's important that people really like their furniture and that what they acquire is indeed useable." He says that all collectors get caught now and then. "I bought this beautiful French hand-carved Regency bench, and when I got it home I found a 'made in Italy' on its underside. It's still a great piece, though, and I'm happy with it."

Lutton is another of those experts who considers it of great importance that the collector only purchase what he really enjoys. He points out that often the market for certain pieces may soften or that a certain style may go out of vogue for a period of time, which means the collector must either be satisfied to hold it until the price comes back or sell for a loss. "I think people make a great mistake when they buy with the profit motive foremost in their minds," he says. "Profit comes because you purchase beautifully tasteful pieces that continue to increase in value, and all the while you are enjoying the great added benefit of possessing a home with marvelous appointments."

He adds, "I think prices today are too high. A person should not buy a piece unless he can afford it without batting an eye. I'd recommend that a person try to get a jump on the other collectors. Right now everyone is after the French and English antiques or the period pieces that fit in with the nostalgia romance. I'd go back a generation or so before the Art Nouveau or Art Deco, to that era encompassing World War I."

But even those pieces are jumping in price too, though they are still relatively cheap. Knight says that golden-oak furniture made near the turn of the century has tripled in value in just more than a year, and that followed a solid increase in value that dates back several years. In the past five years or so, some of these pieces have increased by tenfold. On the East Coast, pine furniture is zooming upward too. Sabbadini says the round oak tables you could buy for $100 or $200 just a couple of years ago are now worth between $700 and $1,000. The big S-shaped roll-top desks that had been about $250 three years ago are now worth between $1,000 and $1,500.

But all of these huge price increases have come in pieces that are extremely popular. Says Schreiber, "The Edwardian craze is a craze. To make it even crazier, the oak furniture is now higher priced than mahogany, and oak is a wood vastly inferior to mahogany for carving, polishability, grain, lustre . . ."

So the collector has a number of considerations in deciding which of the antiques or collectibles to purchase. As there are certain securities more likely to yield steady but relatively unspectacular gains, there are others that possess some kind of a chance for huge gains; in the field of antiques, the same holds true. But in this broad area of collecting the purchaser really has no ground rules to follow, no price-to-earnings ratio or book value for given stocks. He has only his knowledge and the opinion of other experts, and in the case of the dealer who would sell him an item, the opinion of that dealer who stands to profit on the transaction. That means, naturally, that the collector must take steps to provide for his own protection and recourse, if it turns out his purchase is not precisely what he believed he was paying for, or if he, in fact, paid three prices for it.

But in many of these fields of collectibles and would-be antiques—would-be if they were another 30 or even 65 years old—the value of the purchase is not great enough to warrant the use of an appraiser. Many appraisers counsel that if the item is not worth $500 or $1,000, the fee might not be warranted. They do not counsel, however, that the collector just blithely purchase unwarily. "Knowledge is power," says Schreiber. "Knowledge is profit," says Knight. "Knowledge is the buyers only protection," says Lutton. Says yet another appraiser, "Buy a rabbit's foot first."

Still, the collector's best resource continues to be the reputable and able dealer—both are essential qualities. "Every item should be unconditionally warranted as described in the price ticket and there should be a money-back agreement," says Schreiber. "The dealer's obligations also include pointing out all flaws, repairs, weaknesses, restorations, or anything that might tend to decrease value." Adds Ruth Murphy, "Believe nothing oral and only part of what is written."

This skeptic's view of dealers is widely held by appraisers. "Many dealers of limited knowledge offer to appraise only to be able to buy cheaper," says another appraiser. Yet another adds, "Dealers most often simply buy wholesale and slap on a standard 50 to 100 per cent markup. Their ignorance of their merchandise is exceeded only by that of their customers."

The cautions can seem endless. For example, prices are normally higher in resort areas, unless the dealer is caught short of cash before the season opens when he needs to increase inventory or is looking to clear his shelves following the season. Collecting requires insight and knowledge, but it also requires business ability, just like the operation of Macy's and Gimbles, says June Fritch. Collecting also has a few dodges the collector should be aware of. If the collector is at all serious about building his collection, he should naturally become a dealer, which will give him access, at times, to wholesale prices and an added stature among other collectors and professionals in his area.

It might be a good point to reread the tabulated sections in Chapter Two that list many of the items that the experts now consider to be peaking in price and those items or areas of collecting that the experts see as the "hot" new fads, crazes, or fashions. Says Ruth Murphy, "Looking back at my career as a dealer, I see where I made the most money was when I decided 'to take a fling' because I felt some item would become much more in demand."

That is what San Antonio's Moran did with Depression glass, and it is where the collector has the best chance of making big money in a hurry. It is speculation in the truest sense of the word for there is risk that the tin can market, for example, might never materialize.

Some people view "limited editions" as speculations and opportunities for profit, but these people are not knowledgeable collectors. "It's the biggest sucker's game," says one appraiser. "Those 'limited editions' are without exception limited only by the number that can be sold."

On the other hand, most experts agree that the authenticated antiques—those items more than 100 years-old—are among the most solid investments any person can make. Again, the advice suggests that the collector should strive to buy items of quality and taste that were highly prized when they were produced. Both of these standards—quality and taste—are quite often difficult to define, and though all collectors should work to continually improve their own standards, the definition of those qualities concerning specific items is certainly a reason for calling in a professional appraiser.

Still, the final word about buying antiques has to be about the fashion or vogue that creates the demand of a great number of buyers. Fashions can change in fine pieces of antiquity as surely as in speculative lines, though the changes in fashion in these areas of rarified value are much slower in developing. Perhaps the best example of how fashion changes is in the paintings by masters, which will be discussed in the next section. But, briefly, there have been entire schools of painting that during one generation commanded top dollar and then are literally unwanted for a second or third generation of collectors. Ultimately, they regain value, but the collector won't be around to reap the thanks of his grandchild.

Paintings

The experts do not push paintings as fine investments, though they allow that big money can be made on them. "Art investing is flying the kite of speculation," says F. Herbert Hoover of San Francisco's Hoover Gallery. "A person should collect art for the esthetic pleasure, to act as a caretaker of the work, because the ultimate goal of collecting is to preserve the work so that it can be shared with others."

There are several types of paintings the collector might pursue. First, of course, are the framed and renowned works by the old masters and the not-so-famous works by their contemporaries; there are the prints, lithographs, etchings, and other graphics by equally well-known artists; there is contemporary art, paintings and graphics; and there is another area that simply encompasses diverse types of art such as that from Africa, other relatively undiscovered sources of art, and perhaps a loose array of other types that have not yet secured a strong, established marketplace.

But there is probably no other area of collecting that has so many knowledgeable experts who argue that paintings are not a good investment. Indeed, the best reason for purchasing any painting or graphic is because of the esthetic pleasure it gives, or even, because of the exultation that may come from owning a piece of art history, a work by a famed artist of yesteryear. Though as many people possibly collect art because of what they think other people may then think of them because of their collections, it's as valid a reason as collecting for the sheer love of the work and the joy of perusing it. For one of the purposes of art is to civilize man and to live in its presence must have an uplifting effect, regardless of the motivation for its purchase.

John Tucker, an appraiser in Houston, Texas, says flatly: "A work of art is conceived in pleasure and it should be viewed in pleasure, and there's no other earthly reason for possessing a work of art. It must be looked at as a work of art." He adds that probably only about 1 per cent of the contemporary paintings being sold these days are worth the asking price and may never be of greater value than when originally sold. "Everyone is painting today, and even though a painter may be popular today, few will have enduring value. There is fashion, fad, and a lot of the follow-the-leader syndrome in art. A buyer must be very careful."

For many reasons contemporary art becomes the most speculative of ventures in collecting. The odds of the investor making out might be very nearly the same as the backer of a Broadway play, and those are reckoned to be one in a 100. But there's always that grand chance of buying a Warhol, Rauschenberg, or Calder before the artist is recognized as one of the bonafide leaders and geniuses of the new school of painting. There can be and will be fine price increases for the best painters in a regional school, but in terms of investment the idea is to worry about the long haul, a return 20 years or more down the road. Pop art most assuredly will not be as greatly in demand during a certain era some years distant as it is today, and if that is the time a collector finds himself pushed by financial necessity to part with pieces of his collection, he'll learn a stiff lesson. There is, of course, that argument that people who collect certain graphics today because they madly love them may still be collecting them in the future, so demand will always persist. To be sure, but increased prices for art, as well as for stocks or any collectible, come because of an increased demand, which in this instance comes from additional collectors.

Gerald Reitlinger's highly respected work that chronicles the price movements of the works of the masters and the major schools of painters through the centuries concludes that art is a poor investment, even if the collector buys the most renowned masters such as Rembrandt and Renoir. Here, the investor/collector has been seen to protect his money against the eroding force of inflation, but he has not gained in true value over the decades. But that collector has made out far better than other collectors who were buying certain "hot" painters of that time, but have been unheard of ever since.

Writes Reitlinger, in explaining why he still discusses certain artists and schools in his third volume, ". . . there arises the question whether certain painters should not be dropped altogether because their names no longer mean anything at all to students and buyers, who have grown up in the post-war era. (For example,) . . . there are all but forgotten names among the 19th century English watercolour school, the successors to Turner, the Barbizon landscapists and the late 19th century realists. Yet these names created salesroom epics in their day, while their decline in the present century contains the ingredients of high drama (and loss) . . . Their present situation is at least a reminder that not all art-hoarding has been an investment." And throughout his book he details examples of where investors have been caught up short. "The choice of works for rediscovery or promotion has been exceedingly capricious," he adds, "and at times even perverse. Those who listen to the siren song of the brokers of art as an investment, should keep in mind and cast an exceedingly wary look in the direction of the salesroom commentators whose enthusiasm grows ever more round-eyed as the price mounts."

Robert Kaller, an appraiser of fine art in Carmel, California, counsels, "Historical art is more susceptible to an investment approach. Contemporary art is a speculation, almost by definition." The message comes through clearly, to buy a beautiful painting is a decision a person must make because he wants to see that work of art in his collection. Says John Klep of Houston, "You would not want to hang stock certificates or real estate deeds on your walls, would you? There is an enjoyment factor in collecting fine art and antiques, and in the contemplation of these things. So one cannot make comparisons between different types of investments except in a totally impersonal way, and I am not competent to do that because, to me, the 'pleasure' dividend is the most important element in collecting."

The purpose of these sections on the different areas of collecting is to help the collector know under what circumstances it is advisable to call in an expert dealer or appraiser, to understand how the markets work, what the different types of pricing might be, and in general how to purchase works of art without being too badly hurt. There are a great many experts in paintings, to be sure, but particularly in the areas of contemporary art there are none who know better than the collector which of the fashions will endure, though they can assist in pointing out the best of a current fashion. Here, the collector must pursue and gain the "wise eye" and then temper it with his best judgment, knowing full well that few modern painters will see their works escalate in value over time.

Dealers sometimes will slash retail prices but they do not like to knock down prices of an artist's work. The painting is usually on consignment with the split ranging from one-third to the artist to perhaps only one-third to the dealer; it all depends upon which of the two is the shrewdest and which of the two has established the reputation. But when a dealer knocks off the retail price, he is, in effect, taking hard-earned money from the artist's mouth. There is, after all, no royalty arrangements in paintings, and the artist only gains monies the first time his work is sold. Says Kaller, "No collector should ask a dealer to discount contemporary art."

Perhaps the hottest market these days is in graphics, lithographs, and other fine prints. For good reason, one of a kind originals are priced out of the range of most collectors. But the market in prints can swing wildly and an artist can gain overnight popularity. Consider the multitude of prints turned out by Maxfield Parrish in the 1930s. Service stations gave them away. Then, in 1970 in San Francisco the prints got hot. At first the shrewd bargain hunters could find original prints for about $25, then $35, and suddenly they were worth $100 each and up. The fad spread and today some of his finer prints are worth huge sums.

There's the phenomena of the Picasso prints, too. Immediately after his death they had a big run but now they have been settling back, and some experts say because of the plethora of his work, it will be years before they again reach the peaks they experienced. Fad, trend, fashion—they all keep popping up.

The only way a dealer can profit is to more fully understand the market than the collector; the only way the collector can profit from his purchases is to at least know as much as most dealers and more than many. Usually price trends are quite well established before most dealers and collectors stumble onto the idea that there has been a shift; the astute collector is one of the first to recognize that change. One way is to watch what certain artists bring at the major auction houses and to notice just how difficult it is to bring the most knowledgeable dealers down off what had once been terribly firm prices.

But in this area it is also important to actually receive what you pay for. The appraiser and the reputable dealer are essential sources for all knowledgeable collectors. As in other fields, the best dealers will guarantee the authenticity of the work. That is, they guarantee that this picture is indeed a Stuart and this print is a Picasso or Dali; that guarantee has nothing to do with value, of course. The dealers who say this is such-and-such and is worth $2,000 today and next year will be worth $5,000, well, they know full well that if that fact were a certainty they would retire and never part with that painting. It is the purchaser who is always looking for the bargain and "discount" who nearly always finds it and then also finds to his dismay that his cheapy is indeed a cheapy. Naturally, the appraiser can safeguard the collector from *caveat emptor* but so can the reputable dealer.

Tucker explains that "most of the fraud in art is of such a small scale that it's not often heard of. The publicity comes when it gets up in the hundreds or thousands of dollars. But the collector has to realize that the only work of art he's entirely safe with is the one he watched produced. Even then, no one really knows who the good painters are today. Modern art can be valuable, though" he adds. "Andy Warhol's still life of absurd flowers sold at auction for $135,000. And some of our current artists will be heavyweights in any age."

In collecting art, it's as essential as in any other area for the collector to work to become exceedingly knowledgeable, something that often occurs naturally as he pursues his tastes in collecting. Eventually the collector will be able to distinguish etchings from aquatints, whether a print is an original or a photographic reproduction, the difference between limited and unlimited editions, artist's proofs, restrikes, and estate signatures. Jeffrey H. Loria writes in *Collecting Original Art* that when a collector buys for investment he should stick with painters in vogue or seemingly just coming into popularity. He gives a few hints to the collector that could serve him in good stead. For example, he says the collector should know Rembrandt clipped the edges of his etchings extremely close while the 19th century runs have wide margins. Collector's marks and stamps can be a fine guarantee of authenticity, too, he adds, explaining that there is a separate art of knowing about these stamped initials, insignias, coats of arms, crests, numbers, and patterns.

Collecting is like so many areas of knowledge. There's that first insight into the field that lets you know your level of information has value and often times people then figure they know how and when to proceed with their collections. But, naturally, the true student soon learns that he'll never be expert enough. After all, as Loria puts it, if he finds an authentic print of Goya's Disasters of War, he must know whether it is of the fine early state that's worth about $125 (in 1965 dollars) or whether it is a result of the Spanish government's restrikes of his plates, which would mean it would be worth $10 to $20.

Henry Cordier gives an additional insight into collecting art. In his talk before the ASA's international conference in 1975, he said, "While art is the product of any of many intentional or unintentional processes which might have been accidental in origin, it has become a necessary factor in our life to lift us above the daily hunt for food, shelter, and the adjuncts required by our civilization. Art is a highly personal matter to the viewer. As the French artist, Marcel DuChamp said in 1910: 'Art is defined by context and completed by the response of the spectator.' It is an acquired taste that requires knowledge. It is a one-to-one experience, a contemplative pastime. Therefore, a product of artistic effort causes the civilized portion of the world's population to pay more than the usual attention to the respective art work, both the original and its reproductions will be in demand by the public. Somebody in financial or political power will want the original and fight for it, whether with money or with political force. The infamous field marshal, Hermann Goering, of World War II fame, acquired a remarkable art collection with the help of the German army. More than 200 years prior to this, Johann Bottger invented the western equivalent of true procelain at a laboratory of the king of Saxony in Meissen. As a reward for his invention and labors, the king kept him a virtual prisoner for a number of years in order to prevent the secret of making porcelain from leaking out.

"The rest of the population will buy copies, made either by the artist, such as parts of a numbered issue, or they will buy reproductions by the millions created by mercantile enterprises. A good example in this respect is the well-known landscape painter, Robert Wood, still alive in Bishop, California, at this writing, whose landscapes recently have averaged $20,000 for the originals. But, he happens to be one of the most copyrighted and reproduced artists in the world, with every mailman or factory worker admiring the prints of his peaceful landscapes in their livingrooms or dens . . . A few other examples of unusual popularity would be Rembrandt's Man with a Golden Helmet, the Mona Lisa, or, in another medium, one of the countless images and sculptures of Buddha."

Cordier's point is well taken. There is a level of art collecting for every man. What is essential, however, is that the purchaser risk money commensurate with his knowledge. If, for example, a young father of two comes into an inheritance, it makes little sense for him to blow it on one painting, for which he might pay hundreds or thousands of dollars, only to find the painting is decreasing in value, he doesn't like it ultimately, or, even worse, it isn't the painting at all that he thought he was buying.

Of course, the pursuit of paintings and prints affords the collector the rare opportunity of finding the bargain, the discarded rarity. Then, collecting becomes profitable. San Francisco's Hoover tells of finding for $1 a Thomas Hart Benton lithograph that was worth about $200. There are other examples, too, and in such instances much of the risk is removed from collecting. But these kinds of bargains aren't for everyone, because if the collector who finds the "possibly" valuable piece can't cash in on it right then, he stands to lose the opportunity. He must have the knowledge, the eye, the acquired taste to know right there and then that this piece is worth buying.

Many collectors can go a lifetime without having such luck, particularly when they seek valuable works. And generally the rule remains, buying art is *caveat emptor*; there's always a risk. Get the dealer to guarantee in writing the authenticity of the work, get an appraiser when in doubt or when huge sums are involved, attempt to become exceedingly knowledgeable, consult other collectors, frequent museums, find the most reputable dealers, and specialize in an area of art that is most pleasing, exciting, and intriguing. The narrower the field, the more likely the collector is to become knowledgeable—and that is the most important factor of them all.

Books Count, Too

A folio of Audubon's birds sells for $150,000. Old English Georgian parchment sheets, which sold for $15 or $20 each about 12 years ago, today bring from $100 to $150 each. Lossing's two-volume work, *Field Book of the Revolution,* was worth about $12 six years ago; today it's worth more than $100. Copies of the Gutenburg Bible and the Bay Psalm Book—the first book published in the colonies in the 1600s—are priceless. All of them are now in museums or collections destined for museums.

Age alone doesn't make a book valuable. "Many people have a family Bible from the 1800s and they expect it to possess value," says Thelma Fletcher, an appraiser-dealer in rare books in Salado, Texas. "You must remember that the Bible has been printed countless numbers of times. Sure, some of them are valuable. For example, the 'wicked' Bible is, because that version had a misprint, omitting the word 'not' in the adultery commandment." Her point is that in collecting books, as in collecting coins or antiques, it is not necessarily age that counts, because shoddy worksmanship a century ago is still hardly in demand today. It is, again, the best of the rare that is most in demand.

Mrs. Fletcher counsels the collector of rare books to specialize, to collect everything—in the first edition, if possible—of one author, one field, one historical epoch, one binder: "The works of James Joyce and Gertrude Stein have had great revivals. Some of Joyce's signed, limited editions are worth more than $1,500." His manuscripts, naturally, are worth much more. Still, fiction generally is not a great collectors' item. First editions of Ernest Hemingway, William Faulkner, and John Steinbeck can still be purchased for as little as $10 or $15. An autographed set of first editions of the work of

Mark Twain languished with a book seller in Texas for more than a year—he was asking $1,500.

The condition of a book determines its value, and many collectors will never open their rarest volumes, to protect their bindings. "Collectors want books in pristine condition," she says. "There are a lot of collectors who buy only because of the publishing house and others who seek only the beautiful bindings and vellum paper. Anything that did something historically to the country or a part of the country's literature is a sound basis for a collection," she adds, explaining that books on Texas and California are among the most highly sought.

Many book dealers also handle autographs, and descriptions of the manner in which autographs, manuscripts, and various editions of books came about are indeed intriguing. The foremost dealers, when offering a prized collection or an accumulation of prized items for sale, publish a catalogue of the sale or auction. These volumes can be both beautiful and instructive. A few years ago John Howell Books put out a catalogue that included "the very rare autograph of America's most famous pioneer." The description of the autograph and the circumstances surrounding it are exemplary of how detailed the better catalogues can be. The Howell catalogue description: "Boone, Daniel. A.D.s., 1 p., oblong 4 to (2¼x8¼ inches; 6 x 21 cm.); (Kentucky) November 1, 1781. Receipt made out to David Davis. A little stained, tear down the middle carefully repaired. Preserved in a red cloth case. $1,-750. [That was in 1970 and today the autograph would be worth several thousand dollars.] Text as follows: "November the first 1781 / Rcd. of David Davis 7 Dolers in spec(i)e to pay / the Nesecerry Espences of 2 500 akers / Warrants I say Rcd. by me Daniel Boone."

The catalogue adds: "At the time he wrote this receipt the famed pioneer and Indian fighter, who was just turning 47, was living in the settlement he founded and called Boone's Station, and serving as lieutenant-colonel of Fayette County, one of the three counties into which Kentucky was then divided. Six months earlier, in the spring of 1781, he had been chosen by the settlers as their delegate to the state legislature of Virginia (of which Kentucky was then part). In 1782 he was made sheriff and deputy surveyor, in which position it was usual to collect money from settlers for the purchase of land warrants (on a journey east in 1780 to secure such warrants he was robbed of the $20,000 he had collected).

"Daniel Boone autographs are of great rarity. The present example is characteristic of the phonetic spelling used by a man of virtually no formal education. The script, however, is quite legible and the signature is exhibited in full, rather than in the abbreviated form of 'dal Boone' or 'Boon' he sometimes used."

The same Howell catalogue offered "the only complete copy of the first volume of the first California newspaper," which includes copies from August 1846 to May 1847. The newspaper was published in Monterey and was mostly filled with news of the Mexican War, reprints of the works of Melville and Dickens, and of local affairs. It was offered for $29,500. These catalogues become collectors' items themselves.

There was a time when rare books were more in vogue than paintings, any objets d'art, or coins or stamps. Yet today books are not so important, if only because so many of the rarest volumes are no longer available to the collector. This century they have not been the trend setter that they were earlier, and it's unlikely they will be again. Too many of the rarest works cannot be collected; the institutions have them. Yet, they remain of great value, beauty, and interest. The market is strong, vital, and increasing in value by about 25 per cent annually.

It is, of course, an extremely difficult area in which to become expert because of the great numbers of books, to say nothing of the numbers of areas. "You must find a dealer whom you can trust to give you proper advice," says Mrs. Fletcher. "Remember, too, that a book does not have to be old. The Sierra Club books, for example, will become highly prized collectors' items because they are beautifully done and selected with great discrimination. You can and should collect books published today that will give you a very valuable collection within 20 years.''

Books, like many collectibles, are both difficult to find and difficult to sell. To find the buyer at the price you want is often extremely hard, unless the books are to be placed for sale at auction. Some rare books still have not reached the prices they commanded in the boom in rare books in the 1920s. Indeed, the general field of rare books has never fully come back from that peak; its popularity as a collector's item is still relatively restricted. Still, most experts agree that the appreciation in the price of rare books in the years of the last couple of decades have been about 20 to 30 per cent per year. The collecting of rare books is yet another of the many specialized areas in which a person should not enter without the interest and time to become knowledgeable. After all, there was a time, before the electronic media, that books were of the greatest value and, regardless of a book's age, it could command a premium simply because it offered information available from no other source. Today that premium has a diminished value, but the beautifully bound and rare works continue to be in great demand.

Profit and Pleasure

There was a wonderful, white-haired gentleman, Cornelius MacMillan, who lived cater-corner from where I grew up in Topeka. On Sundays I would cut his grass, he'd pay me fifty cents, and every once-in-awhile he'd throw in an Indian head penny. I was 13 and had just begun sacking groceries on Saturdays, and too, rummaging through the cash register for old coins—Buffalo nickels, Liberty standing quarters, even some silver dollars. Often, after cutting Mr. Mac's grass, he'd invite me into his house where he'd pull some of his coin collection out of his strongbox.

One day he asked me if I'd been saving my money because he had just gone through his collection and found a number of extraneous coins. At first I thought he was talking about fairly common duplicates, but, no, he had a selection of 21 U.S. coins dating back to 1801. We bargained for more than an hour and I remember paying him $21.83 for the coins, marveling at how shrewdly I'd handled the transaction. After all, the coins' book value then was about $35.

But I was puzzled. It seemed that any really old coin should fit into any coin collection. I don't recall Mr. Mac's precise words, but I remember clearly his explanation that a jumble of old coins is not a collection but a "jumble of old coins." A collection is something you build, work to complete, construct, and becomes more valuable for your efforts, he said. And then he pulled from his strongbox glittering collections of silver dollars, large cents, small cents, even the golden double eagles. That was a collection, not a smattering of old coins.

There's more glory to a collection than how wonderfully it appears: A collection reflects much of the collector. It says things about the individual's innovativeness, genius, imagination, taste, persistence, and understanding. A collection can achieve historical importance and it can add to our knowledge. The collector becomes historian, anthropologist, and archeologist, and in the process perhaps gives us a unique view of some part of our past. Today, for example, pieces that might have been in the Getty or Simon collections have added stature and value because those collectors had at one time prized them highly.

A warning: collecting can become a passion. If the beginning collector chooses his area wisely, finds a field that will amaze, interest, and intrigue him, and knows the pleasure of becoming absorbed in his pursuit—well, his life will be dramatically changed. He'll become a person in demand for his expertise. That, of course, is one of the pleasureable benefits, a benefit too, that can lead to sometimes as much profit as his collecting activities themselves.

So the goal is not merely to purchase an item, hold it for a year or five, and sell it for a profit. There's hardly a thing wrong with that. And so long as that process works, fine. But if a person chooses that path he will inevitably remain only as successful as his advisors—and his good fortune. What's essential is to select a procedure, a process that will finally provide enough insight and knowledge so that purchases can be made at the proper time, with quality and value properly accounted for, and in the field of expertise that's been acquired.

Esthetic pleasure. The pursuit of beauty and art. The custodian of the past. All of the grand reasons for collecting are valuable but pale if the profit isn't there. Profit and pleasure. Sure, profit nearly always means pleasure these days so it's probably the best way to insure that the collection has meaning and pleasure.

There are best buys today. Oriental rugs have no direction to move but straight up. The demand is much greater than the supply. The oil-rich Sheiks even come to this country these days seeking the best rugs, and American interest has never been higher. "Nothing in life is certain," says one appraiser, "but death, taxes, and rising values in Oriental rugs."

What we're talking about, however, is a process, a procedure, a game plan. A strategy that will pay handsomely.

The key is to collect items in a field that you've already proven to yourself to hold your interest. If it's gold, fine. Firearms. The finely tuned mechanism of the automotive engine. The glory of works by the old masters. Kitchen implements. Any of them work, but always work to narrow your area of growing expertise until you become if not "the" expert, at least one of the experts.

Read, research, and study. Knowledge equals profit. Know why a certain period of english history produced that intricate craftsmanship we now call Victoriana. Or why furniture turned so austere in pattern in another age. History is an honorable pursuit.

Become a hunter—of value and quality. Handle the items at auctions, in dealers' showrooms, at flea markets. Know the feel of fine porcelain, the smoothness of marble, the patina of age, the curve of true genius in sculpture. And spend money acquiring knowledge.

Buy only what you can afford to hang onto comfortably. The fastest road to rags is to buy items that are too expensive and then, because of illness or unemployment, to be forced to sell them quickly. It's as difficult to make a good sale as to negotiate a good buy. So always purchase only items that greatly please you, items you'll love to own and keep until the profit and opportunity for turning the profit arise.

Expect and demand authentication. It's essential to work to reduce the hazards of caveat emptor—buyer beware. Know that your purchase is either the real thing or, if you can prove it is not, you'll get your money back. The best dealers will readily agree to that bargain. Frequent auctions but realize they are the pits and arenas of the pros, that many times people bid and buy objects for reasons other than monetary value. They may be collectors who need an item to complete a collection, damn the price. Still the auction is the bread and butter of collecting so know how they work and get ready to join into the bidding when your expert knowledge arrives.

Trade up from the good to the best, try to use your profits to build your collection. If you aren't turning a profit, it should tell you a few other people know too much more than you. And don't get taken. Beware of the fakery and the forgery.

Hobnob with the experts. Join clubs and associations. Help others and they'll return the favor. But always remember that all collectors are after the same thing—the grand collection, the big profit, the esthetic pleasure. No one is going to give you a deal.

There are no shortcuts to knowledge, yet figure on paying an appraiser or dealer for help—it's cheap at the price. If a collector pursues his field with enough persistence, inevitably he'll one-day become an expert. Finally, the best advice is that the old stock-market trader passes on, buy low and sell high. But if you learn you bought too high, sell fast at a kind-of high price. Don't hold onto your mistakes, but eat your losses and move onto another purchase that can help you recoup.

The thrust of this book is straight enough. If you will find an area that you love, you'll spend enough time with it to become one of the knowledgeable few, which certainly means profit in the longhaul. It's an exciting prospect. I recall one experience in an old town in the goldfields of the Sierra Nevada mountains in California. The shop was a musty collection of old farm implements, a few pieces of brass, and some furniture. I had picked up an old picture in what appeared to be an older frame. I liked its appearance, feel, and color, but the dealer there wanted $25 for it. She knew nothing about it and neither did I. About then, I noticed another lady moving through the store but paid her little mind. Finally, I put the picture down and started to move on. The other lady was there like a vulture, grabbing it and holding $25 out to the dealer. A few minutes later I walked out to my car. She was sitting with her husband and they were convulsed in laughter. As their car backed out, she yelled at me, "It's worth thousands." Maybe she knew and perhaps she didn't. I can tell you, however, it destroyed any pleasure I felt for my efforts that day, and for certain, that lady, sure in her knowledge, was at least for the moment loving the pleasure her profit had given her. I hope it's my turn soon—and yours.